核心素养英语阅读系列

总主编：林敦来　郭乙瑶

科学素养英语阅读

主编
林敦来　赵胜杰

编者
张庆霞　于静蕾
孙　悦　王永莹

Selected Readings in Science

清华大学出版社
北京

内 容 简 介

本书参照国际通用的科学教育内容标准,包含科学概念与过程、科学探究、物理、生命科学、地球与空间科学、科技、科学以及科学的历史与本质等。本书共 10 个单元,每个单元分为 Text A 和 Text B,共 20 篇文章。本书充分实现了内容和语言相融合的教学理念,在有效提升学生英语语言能力的同时,还有助于培养学生的科学探究精神以及批判和创新思维意识,从而助力科技创新人才的培养。本书每个单元配套单元小测验,读者可先扫描封底的"文泉云盘防盗码"解锁资源后,再扫描书中对应处的二维码获取资源,登录清华大学出版社"文泉考试"平台进行线上测验。

本书可作为本科高年级及研究生英语阅读类课程的主干教材,也可作为通识类选修课程的教材,还可以作为对科学感兴趣,又希望切实提高英语水平的学生的课外读物。

版权所有,侵权必究。举报: 010-62782989, beiqinquan@tup.tsinghua.edu.cn。

图书在版编目(CIP)数据

科学素养英语阅读 / 林敦来,郭乙瑶总主编;林敦来等主编. -- 北京:清华大学出版社,2024.7.
(核心素养英语阅读系列). -- ISBN 978-7-302-66718-6

I. H319.37

中国国家版本馆 CIP 数据核字第 20246DX038 号

责任编辑:徐博文
封面设计:李伯骥
责任校对:王荣静
责任印制:刘 菲

出版发行:清华大学出版社
网　　址:https://www.tup.com.cn, https://www.wqxuetang.com
地　　址:北京清华大学学研大厦 A 座　　邮　编:100084
社 总 机:010-83470000　　邮　购:010-62786544
投稿与读者服务:010-62776969, c-service@tup.tsinghua.edu.cn
质量反馈:010-62772015, zhiliang@tup.tsinghua.edu.cn

印 装 者:北京嘉实印刷有限公司
经　　销:全国新华书店
开　　本:185mm×260mm　　印　张:13.25　　字　数:281 千字
版　　次:2024 年 9 月第 1 版　　印　次:2024 年 9 月第 1 次印刷
定　　价:59.00 元

产品编号:105334-01

前　言

党的二十大报告指出，"教育、科技、人才是全面建设社会主义现代化国家的基础性、战略性支撑。必须坚持科技是第一生产力、人才是第一资源、创新是第一动力，深入实施科教兴国战略、人才强国战略、创新驱动发展战略，开辟发展新领域新赛道，不断塑造发展新动能新优势。"这足以突显科技发展和创新在我国全面建设社会主义现代化进程中占据举足轻重的地位。科学创新与发展是推动现代社会进步的原动力。在我国建设科技强国这样的大时代背景下，本教程应运而生。

本教程精选的 20 篇文章综合体现了我国科学课程要培养的学生发展核心素养，即科学观念、科学思维、探究实践、态度责任。编者在选材时参考了国际通用的科学教育内容标准，包含科学概念与过程、科学探究、物理、生命科学、地球与空间科学、科技、科学的个人视角和社会视角以及科学历史与本质八个方面。这八个方面精心地渗透于教程的 10 个单元中。第一单元 "Approaching Science" 通过概览现代科学历史为读者解开科学之谜，并以科技对人类产生的影响，激发读者思考科学与人类命运的关系；第二单元 "Science Literacy" 针对科学素养普及的难点，呈现了一个新文科视阈下 "设情境、提问题、探究竟" 的科学课堂，以期让学生爱上科学课，同时也探究科学素养的本质和重要性及其提升策略；第三单元 "Chemical Science" 以化学之美妙衬托几位优秀的化学家，体现科学的个人视角；第四单元 "Science as Inquiry" 紧紧围绕 "探究" 这一关键词，呈现探究的多重形式，深化学生对科学探究过程的认识；第五单元 "Science as Human Endeavor" 探讨了科学研究与人类行为之间的复杂关系，阐明执着、勤奋而严谨的治学求真精神以及社会因素对于科学研究的重要性；第六至第九单元分别从物理、生命科学、地球与空间科学、科技方面，让学生感受科学的奥妙；第十单元 "Science: Past and Future" 在阐明现代生物学的发展离不开达尔文影响的同时，强调想象力、人类需求和提出新问题等诸因素对推动科学创新和发展发挥的至关重要的作用。

本教程是在新文科视角下，在传统文科的基础上，融合了现代科学和技术的阅读教程。它突破了传统文科对文化、历史、文学等学科范畴的限制，更加关注跨学科的研究和应用。新文科将不同学科的知识进行整合，形成新的研究领域，这种跨学科研究成为新文科的一大特点。借鉴这一新视角，本教程跨越英语学习和科学知识两者之间的学科壁垒，让学生在阅读英文的基础上自然习得语言和科学知识，可谓一箭双雕，一举多得。

通过系统性的内容呈现，本教程充分体现了内容和语言相融合的教学理念，在提升学生英语阅读能力的同时，通过科学的概念、方法和程序的复现逐步培养学生用英语讲科学故事的能力。本教程还特别注重科学探究精神的培养，每篇文章后面设置了8-9个问题，既包含阅读理解题，也包含思维拓展题，在确保学生掌握不同科学知识的同时，还可以培养学生的批判和创新思维意识，从而有效地助力科技创新人才的培养。本教程既可作为本科高年级及研究生英语阅读类课程的主干教材，也可作为通识类选修课程的教材，还可以让对科学感兴趣，又希望切实提高英语水平的学生作为课外读物使用。在课堂教学中，教师应鼓励学生在课前积极完成导入问题，了解相关背景信息，为阅读理解做必要的背景知识准备。在学习课文时，教师应以理解意义为主要教学任务，附带语言教学。每个单元的习题从信息类到阐释类，让学生联系实际发表看法类问题，认知层层递进。

北京师范大学外国语言文学学院对本教程的出版给予了大力支持，外籍教师 Eric Howald 对本教程进行了仔细审读，清华大学出版社的编辑团队对本教程进行了细致的审稿与编校，编者在此一并表示感谢。本教程经历四年多的选材，几易其稿，以追求精益求精，但编者团队均系英语语言文学和应用语言学的学科背景，对科学领域知识的了解仍是皮毛。因此本教程尚存在诸多不足之处，恳请读者为我们提出宝贵建议，以便再版时改进。衷心感谢。

编　者
2024 年 7 月

Contents

Unit 1	**Approaching Science** 1
Text A	What Is Science 3
Text B	Science and Human Life 12

Unit 2	**Science Literacy** 21
Text A	Freshman Chemistry Was Never Like This 24
Text B	Scientific Literacy: What It Is, Why It's Important, and Why We don't Have It 32

Unit 3	**Chemical Science** 41
Text A	Tiny Pieces of Matter 43
Text B	Chemistry Way, Way Below Zero 51

Unit 4	**Science as Inquiry** 59
Text A	A Brief History of Inquiry: From Dewey to Standards 61
Text B	Inquiry in Science and in Classrooms 70

Unit 5	**Science as Human Endeavor** 81
Text A	The Humble Scientist 83
Text B	Vindicating Science—By Bringing It Down 90

Unit 6	**Physical Science** 99
Text A	The Big Bang 102
Text B	The Structure of Physics 111

iii

Unit 7 Life Science 125

Text A   Human Biological Adaptability 127
Text B   Tracing the Origins of Humans 136

Unit 8 Earth and Space Science 145

Text A   How Did Earth and Other Planets Form? 147
Text B   The Age of Earth 156

Unit 9 Science and Technology 165

Text A   Artificial Intelligence 167
Text B   The Measured Life 176

Unit 10 Science: Past and Future 187

Text A   The End of Evolutionary Biology 189
Text B   Science Especially About the Future 197

Approaching Science

Synopsis

"什么是科学"这个问题看似容易，但回答起来却相当困难。从哲学角度看，科学是科学家运用实验法、观察法和理论架构来解开自然之谜的行为。人类创造的科学技术正以愈加快速的方式改变着人类的生活。人类能否适应科学所带来的所有变化？科技从业者应该承担怎样的社会责任？这些问题至今仍未有明晰的答案。本单元 Text A 通过概览现代科学历史为读者解开科学之谜；Text B 分析科技对人类产生的影响，激发读者思考科学与人类命运的关系。

Warm-up

Below are some famous scientists. Identify his or her invention or discovery. Draw lines to match the scientists with their inventions or discoveries. In your opinion, which invention or discovery is the greatest? Why?

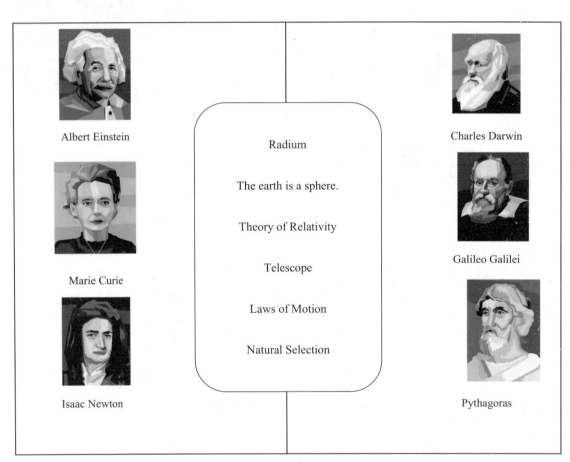

Text A

Background information

This article is extracted from *Philosophy of Science: A Very Short Introduction*, which was published by Oxford University Press in 2002. The book was authored by Samir Okasha, Professor of Philosophy of Science, University of Bristol. It delves into the historical and contemporary challenges of the philosophy of science, covering the core debates and deals with key questions such as the issue of scientific change. The second edition was released in 2016. This extract is the beginning of the 2002 edition which gives a short history of science.

What Is Science

Samir Okasha

What is science? This question may seem easy to answer: everybody knows that subjects such as physics, chemistry, and biology constitute science, while subjects such as art, music, and theology do not. But when as philosophers we ask what science is, that is not the sort of answer we want. We are not asking for a mere list of the activities that are usually called "science". Rather, we are asking what common feature all the things on that list share, i.e. what it is that *makes* something a science. Understood this way, our question is not so **trivial**.

But you may still think the question is relatively straightforward. Surely science is just the attempt to understand, explain, and predict the world we live in? This is certainly a reasonable answer. But is it the whole story? After all, the various religions also attempt to understand and explain the world, but religion is not usually regarded as a branch of science. Similarly, **astrology** and fortune-telling are attempts to predict the future, but most people would not describe these activities as science. Or consider history. Historians try to understand and explain what happened in the past, but history is usually classified as an arts subject not a science subject. As with

trivial 不重要的，没有价值的

astrology 占星术

many philosophical questions, the question "what is science?" turns out to be trickier than it looks at first sight.

Many people believe that the distinguishing features of science lie in the particular *methods* scientists use to investigate the world. This suggestion is quite **plausible**. For many sciences do employ distinctive methods of enquiry that are not found in non-scientific disciplines. An obvious example is the use of experiments, which historically marks a turning-point in the development of modern science. Not all the sciences are experimental though—astronomers obviously cannot do experiments on the heavens, but have to content themselves with careful observation instead. The same is true of many social sciences. Another important feature of science is the construction of theories. Scientists do not simply record the results of experiment and observation in a **log** book—they usually want to explain those results in terms of a general theory. This is not always easy to do, but there have been some striking successes. One of the key problems in philosophy of science is to understand how techniques such as experimentation, observation, and theory construction have enabled scientists to **unravel** so many of nature's secrets.

The origins of modern science

In today's schools and universities, science is taught in a largely **ahistorical** way. Textbooks present the key ideas of a scientific discipline in as convenient a form as possible, with little mention of the lengthy and often **tortuous** historical process that led to their discovery. As a pedagogical strategy, this makes good sense. But some appreciation of the history of scientific ideas is helpful for understanding the issues that interest philosophers of science. Indeed, it has been argued that close attention to the history of science is indispensable for doing good philosophy of science.

The origins of modern science lie in a period of rapid scientific development that occurred in Europe between the years 1500 and 1750, which we now refer to as the *Scientific Revolution*. Of course, scientific investigations were pursued in ancient and medieval times too—the scientific revolution did not come from nowhere. In these

---

plausible 貌似有道理的

log 日志

unravel 解开、澄清

ahistorical 与历史无关的
tortuous 曲折的

earlier periods the dominant worldview was **Aristotelianism**, named after the ancient Greek philosopher Aristotle, who put forward detailed theories in physics, biology, astronomy, and cosmology. But Aristotle's ideas would seem very strange to a modern scientist, as would his methods of enquiry. To pick just one example, he believed that all earthly bodies are composed of just four elements: earth, fire, air, and water. This view is obviously at odds with what modern chemistry tells us.

The first crucial step in the development of the modern scientific worldview was the Copernican revolution. In 1542 the Polish astronomer **Nicolas Copernicus** (1473—1543) published a book attacking the geocentric model of the universe, which placed the stationary earth at the centre of the universe with the planets and the sun in orbit around it. Geocentric astronomy, also known as Ptolemaic astronomy after the ancient Greek astronomer Ptolemy, lay at the heart of the Aristotelian worldview, and had gone largely unchallenged for 1,800 years. But Copernicus suggested an alternative: the sun was the fixed centre of the universe, and the planets, including the earth, were in orbit around the sun. On this heliocentric model the earth is regarded as just another planet, and so loses the unique status that tradition had accorded it. Copernicus' theory initially met with much resistance, not least from the Catholic Church who regarded it as **contravening** the Scriptures and in 1616 banned books advocating the earth's motion. But within 100 years Copernicanism had become established scientific **orthodoxy**.

Copernicus' innovation did not merely lead to a better astronomy. Indirectly, it led to the development of modern physics, through the work of **Johannes Kepler** (1571—1630) and Galileo Galilei (1564—1642). Kepler discovered that the planets do not move in circular orbits around the sun, as Copernicus thought, but rather in *ellipses*. This was his crucial "first law" of planetary motion; his second and third laws specify the speeds at which the planets orbit the sun.

Taken together, Kepler's laws provided a far superior planetary theory than had ever been advanced before, solving problems that had confounded astronomers for centuries. Galileo was a life-long supporter of Copernicanism, and one of the early pioneers of the

Aristotelianism
亚里士多德主义，受亚里士多德著作启发而成立的哲学传统，在研究自然和自然规律时以演绎逻辑和分析归纳为主要特征。

Nicolas Copernicus
尼古拉·哥白尼，现代天文学之父，是文艺复兴时期的波兰天文学家、数学家、教会法博士和神父；提出了日心说，改变了人类对自然和对自身的看法。
contravene 违反；与……有冲突
orthodoxy 普遍接受的观点，正统观点

Johannes Kepler
约翰尼斯·开普勒，德国天文学家、数学家与占星家。他发现了行星运动三大定律：轨道定律、等面积定律和周期定律。

telescope. When he pointed his telescope at the heavens, he made a wealth of amazing discoveries, including mountains on the moon, a vast array of stars, sun-spots, and Jupiter's moons. All of these conflicted thoroughly with Aristotelian cosmology, and played a **pivotal** role in converting the scientific community to Copernicanism.

Galileo's most enduring contribution, however, lay not in astronomy but in mechanics, where he **refuted** the Aristotelian theory that heavier bodies fall faster than lighter ones. In place of this theory, Galileo made the counter-intuitive suggestion that all freely falling bodies will fall towards the earth at the same rate, irrespective of their weight. (Of course in practice, if you drop a feather and a cannon-ball from the same height the cannonball will land first, but Galileo argued that this is simply due to air resistance—in a vacuum, they would land together.) Furthermore, he argued that freely falling bodies accelerate uniformly, i.e. gain equal **increments** of speed in equal times; this is known as Galileo's law of free-fall. Galileo provided persuasive though not totally conclusive evidence for this law, which formed the centrepiece of his theory of mechanics.

Galileo is generally regarded as the first truly modern physicist. He was the first to show that the language of mathematics could be used to describe the behaviour of actual objects in the material world, such as falling bodies, **projectiles**, etc. To us this seems obvious—today's scientific theories are routinely formulated in mathematical language, not only in the physical sciences but also in biology and economics. But in Galileo's day it was not obvious: mathematics was widely regarded as dealing with purely abstract entities, and hence inapplicable to physical reality. Another innovative aspect of Galileo's work was his emphasis on the importance of testing hypotheses experimentally. To the modern scientist, this may again seem obvious. But at the time that Galileo was working, experimentation was not generally regarded as a reliable means of gaining knowledge. Galileo's emphasis on experimental testing marks the beginning of an empirical approach to studying nature that continues to this day.

The period following Galileo's death saw the scientific revolution rapidly gain in momentum. The French philosopher, mathematician,

pivotal 核心的
refute 反驳
increment 增量
projectile 发射物

and scientist **Rene Descartes** (1596—1650) developed a radical new "mechanical philosophy", according to which the physical world consists simply of inert particles of matter interacting and colliding with one another. The laws governing the motion of these particles or "corpuscles" held the key to understanding the structure of the Copernican universe, Descartes believed. The mechanical philosophy promised to explain all observable phenomena in terms of the motion of these inert, insensible corpuscles, and quickly became the dominant scientific vision of the second half of the 17th century; to some extent it is still with us today. Versions of the mechanical philosophy were **espoused**, by figures such as Huygens, Gassendi, Hooke, Boyle, and others; its widespread acceptance marked the final downfall of the Aristotelian worldview.

The scientific revolution **culminated** in the work of Isaac Newton (1643—1727), whose achievements stand unparalleled in the history of science. Newton's masterpiece was his *Mathematical Principles of Natural Philosophy*, published in 1687.

Newton agreed with the mechanical philosophers that the universe consists simply of particles in motion, but sought to improve on Descartes' laws of motion and rules of collision. The result was a dynamical and mechanical theory of great power, based around **Newton's Three Laws of Motion** and his famous principle of *universal gravitation*. According to this principle, everybody in the universe exerts a gravitational attraction on every other body; the strength of the attraction between two bodies depends on the product of their masses, and on the distance between them squared. The laws of motion then specify how this gravitational force affects the bodies' motions. Newton elaborated his theory with great mathematical precision and rigour, inventing the mathematical technique we now call "calculus". Strikingly, Newton was able to show that Kepler's Laws of Planetary Motion and Galileo's Law of Free-Fall (both with certain minor modifications) were logical consequences of his laws of motion and gravitation. In other words, the very same laws would explain the motions of bodies in both **terrestrial** and **celestial** domains, and were formulated by Newton in a precise quantitative form.

Rene Descartes

勒内·笛卡尔，法国哲学家和数学家。他是现代哲学的奠基者之一，1641年出版的《第一哲学沉思录》至今仍是多数大学哲学专业的主干教材之一。

espouse 支持，拥护

culminate 达到顶点

Newton's Three Laws of Motion

牛顿运动三大定律，由牛顿1687年在《自然哲学的数学原理》一书中总结提出。第一定律说明了力的含义：力是改变物体运动状态的原因；第二定律指出了力的作用效果：力使物体获得加速度；第三定律揭示出力的本质：力是物体间的相互作用。

terrestrial 陆地的

celestial 天体的

Newtonian physics provided the framework for science for the next 200 years or so, quickly replacing Cartesian physics. Scientific confidence grew rapidly in this period, due largely to the success of Newton's theory, which was widely believed to have revealed the true workings of nature, and to be capable of explaining everything, in principle at least. Detailed attempts were made to extend the Newtonian mode of explanation to more and more phenomena. The 18th and 19th centuries both saw notable scientific advances, particularly in the study of chemistry, optics, energy, thermodynamics, and electromagnetism. But for the most part, these developments were regarded as falling within a broadly Newtonian conception of the universe. Scientists accepted Newton's conception as essentially correct; all that remained to be done was to fill in the details.

Confidence in the Newtonian picture was **shattered** in the early years of the 20th century, thanks to two revolutionary new developments in physics: relativity theory and quantum mechanics. Relativity theory, discovered by Einstein, showed that Newtonian mechanics does not give the right results when applied to very massive objects, or objects moving at very high **velocities**. Quantum mechanics, conversely, shows that the Newtonian theory does not work when applied on a very small scale, to subatomic particles. Both relativity theory and quantum mechanics, especially the latter, are very strange and radical theories, making claims about the nature of reality that many people find hard to accept or even understand. Their emergence caused considerable conceptual upheaval in physics, which continues to this day.

So far, our brief account of the history of science has focused mainly on physics. This is no accident, as physics is both historically very important, and in a sense, the most fundamental of all scientific disciplines. For the objects that other sciences study are themselves made up of physical entities. Consider botany, for example. Botanists study plants, which are ultimately composed of **molecules** and atoms, which are physical particles. So botany is obviously less fundamental than physics—though that is not to say it is any less important. But even a brief description of modern science's origins would be incomplete if it omitted all mention of the non-physical sciences.

---

shatter 使破碎

velocity 速度

molecule 分子

In biology, the event that stands out is Charles Darwin's discovery of the theory of evolution by natural selection, published in *The Origin of Species* in 1859. Until then it was widely believed that the different species had been separately created by God, as **The Book of Genesis** teaches. But Darwin argued that contemporary species have actually evolved from ancestral ones, through a process known as *natural selection*. Natural selection occurs when some organisms leave more offspring than others, depending on their physical characteristics; if these characteristics are then inherited by their offspring, over time the population will become better and better adapted to the environment. Simple though this process is, over a large number of generations it can cause one species to evolve into a wholly new one, Darwin argued. So persuasive was the evidence Darwin **adduced** for his theory that by the start of the 20th century it was accepted as scientific orthodoxy, despite considerable theological opposition. Subsequent work has provided striking confirmation of Darwin's theory, which forms the centrepiece of the modern biological worldview.

The 20th century witnessed another revolution in biology that is not yet complete: the emergence of molecular biology, in particular molecular genetics. In 1953 **Watson and Crick** discovered the structure of DNA, the hereditary material that makes up the genes in the cells of living creatures. Watson and Crick's discovery explained how genetic information can be copied from one cell to another, and thus passed down from parent to offspring, thereby explaining why offspring tend to resemble their parents. Their discovery opened up an exciting new area of biological research. In the 50 years since Watson and Crick's work, molecular biology has grown fast, transforming our understanding of heredity and of how genes build organisms. The recent attempt to provide a molecular-level description of the complete set of genes in a human being, known as the Human Genome Project, is an indication of how far molecular biology has come. The 21st century will see further exciting developments in this field.

More resources have been devoted to scientific research in the last hundred years than ever before. One result has been an

---

The Book of Genesis
　《创世纪》是希伯来圣经和基督教旧约的第一本书；描述了世界是如何创造的，以及人类的早期历史。

adduce 援引

Watson and Crick
　沃特森和克里克，1953 年发现 DNA 的双螺旋结构，1962 年获诺贝尔奖。他们合著有 *The Double Helix: A Personal Account of the Discovery of the Structure of DNA*；该书叙述了沃特森和克里克如何发现 DNA 双螺旋结构。

explosion of new scientific disciplines, such as computer science, artificial intelligence, linguistics, and neuroscience. Possibly the most significant event of the last 30 years is the rise of cognitive science, which studies various aspects of human cognition such as perception, memory, learning, and reasoning, and has transformed traditional psychology. Much of the impetus for cognitive science comes from the idea that the human mind is in some respects similar to a computer, and thus that human mental processes can be understood by comparing them to the operations computers carry out. Cognitive science is still in its **infancy**, but promises to reveal much about the workings of the mind. The social sciences, especially economics and sociology, have also flourished in the 20th century, though many people believe they still lag behind the natural sciences in terms of sophistication and rigour.	infancy 萌芽阶段
(2,553 words)	

❶ Recall

Answer the following questions with the information from the passage.

1. In what way is astrology and fortune-telling similar to science?
2. How do astronomers study the heavens?
3. What was the dominant worldview of science in ancient and medieval times?
4. What is Galileo's most enduring contribution?
5. What revolution in biology took off in the 20th century?
6. What motivated the birth of cognitive science?

❷ Interpret

Answer the following questions by analysing the passage.

7. At the end of Paragraph 2, the author says, "As with many philosophical questions, the question 'What is science?' turns out to be trickier than it looks at first sight." What features of science distinguish it from other fields of study?
8. How did modern physical science evolve? Name the most important theories of each period and their main contributors.

Unit 1 Approaching Science

Evaluate & Connect

Answer the following question by relating the passage to your own experience.

9. As the world's greatest populariser of science, Carl Sagan said, "Science is a way of thinking much more than it is a body of knowledge." Based on Text A and your own knowledge, make some comments on the quote.

Text B

Background Information

This article is an excerpt from *What is Science? Twelve Eminent Scientists Explain Their Various Fields to the Layman*, edited by James R. Newman and published in 1955 by Simon & Schuster. Addressing the general reader, the book focuses on the nature of scientific knowledge, the scientific method, and science as an intellectual pursuit. This excerpt is authored by Bertrand Russell, a Nobel Prize winner of Literature in 1950. Russell was one of the early 20th century's most prominent philosophers, mathematicians and logicians, and one of the founders of analytic philosophy. He advocated humanitarian ideals and freedom of thought in his writings.

Science and Human Life

Bertrand Russell

Science and the techniques to which it has given rise have changed human life during the last hundred and fifty years more than it had been changed since men **took to** agriculture, and the changes that are being **wrought** by science continue at an increasing speed. There is no sign of any new stability to be attained on some scientific **plateau**. On the contrary, there is every reason to think that the revolutionary possibilities of science extend immeasurably beyond what has so far been realized. Can the human race adjust itself quickly enough to these **vertiginous** transformations, or will it, as innumerable former species have done, perish from lack of adaptability? The dinosaurs were, in their day, the lords of creation, and if there had been philosophers among them not one would have foreseen that the whole race might perish. But they became extinct because they could not adapt themselves to a world without **swamps**. In the case of man and science, there is a wholly new factor, namely that man himself is creating the changes of environment to which he will have to adjust himself with unprecedented rapidity. But,

take to 开始做

wrought 使发生

plateau 平台；高原

vertiginous 引起眩晕的

swamp 沼泽

although man through his scientific skill is the cause of the changes of environment, most of these changes are not willed by human beings. Although they come about **through human agencies**, they have, or at any rate have had so far, something of the **inexorable** inevitability of natural forces. Whether Nature dried up the swamps or men deliberately drained them, makes little difference as regards the ultimate result. Whether men will be able to survive the changes of environment that their own skill has brought about is an open question. If the answer is in the **affirmative**, it will be known some day; if not, not. If the answer is to be in the affirmative, men will have to apply scientific ways of thinking to themselves and their institutions. They cannot continue to hope, as all politicians hitherto have, that in a world where everything has changed, the political and social habits of the eighteenth century can remain **inviolate**. Not only will men of science have to grapple with the sciences that deal with man, but—and this is a far more difficult matter—they will have to persuade the world to listen to what they have discovered. If they cannot succeed in this difficult **enterprise**, man will destroy himself by his halfway cleverness. I am told that, if he were out of the way, the future would lie with rats. I hope they will find it a pleasant world, but I am glad I shall not be there.

  But let us pass from these generalities to more specific questions. One of the most obvious problems raised by a scientific technique is that of the exhaustion of the soil and of raw materials. This subject has been much discussed, and some governments have actually taken some steps to prevent the **denudation** of the soil. But I doubt whether, as yet, the good done by these measures is outweighing the harm done in less careful regions. Food, however, is such an obvious necessity that the problem is bound to receive increasing attention as population pressure makes it more urgent. Whether this increased attention will do good or harm in the long run is, I fear, questionable. By a **spendthrift** use of fertilizers, food production in the present can be increased at the cost of food production in the future. Can you imagine a politician going to his **constituents** and saying: "Ladies and gentlemen, it is in your power to have abundance of food for the next thirty years, but the measures that will give you this abundance

---

through the agency of 由于……的作用

inexorable 不可阻挡的

affirmative 肯定

inviolate 未被违反的

enterprise 事业

denudation 剥蚀

spendthrift 挥霍无度的

constituent 选民

will cause scarcity for your grandchildren. I am therefore proposing measures to ensure frugality in the present in order to avoid famine in the somewhat distant future." Is it possible to believe that a politician who said this would win elections against one less addicted to foresight? I hardly think so, unless the general level of political intelligence and virtue can be very considerably increased.

The question of raw materials is more difficult and complex than the question of food. The raw materials required at one stage of technique are different from those required at another. It may be that by the time the world's supply of oil is exhausted, atomic power will have taken its place. But to this sort of process there is a limit, though not an easily assignable one. At present there is a race for **uranium**, and it would seem likely that before very long there will be no easily accessible source of uranium. If, when that happens, the world has come to depend upon nuclear energy as its main source of power, the result may be devastating. All such speculations are of course very questionable, since new techniques may always make it possible to **dispense with** formerly necessary raw materials. But we cannot get away from the broad fact that we are living upon the world's **capital** of stored energy and are transforming the energy at a continually increasing rate into forms in which it cannot be utilized. Such a manner of life can hardly be stable, but must sooner or later bring the penalty that lies in wait for those who live on capital.

In primitive times, when the human population of the globe was small, such problems did not arise. Agriculture, it is true, was practiced in ways that exhausted the soil for a time, but there were usually new vacant lands available; and if there were not, the corpses of enemies **sufficed** as fertilizers. The system was "conservative" in the physicists' sense. That is to say, energy on the whole accumulated as fast as it was used. Now, this is not the case; and, so far as one can see, it will never be the case while scientific technique continues.

All this however, you may say, is distant and doubtful: we have more pressing matters to consider. This is true, and I will proceed to consider some of them.

The problem which most preoccupies the public mind at the present moment is that of scientific warfare. It has become evident

uranium 铀

dispense with 省掉，摒除

capital 存量，总量

suffice 足够

that, if scientific skill is allowed free scope, the human race will be **exterminated**, if not in the next war, then in the next but one or the next but two—at any rate at no very distant date. To this problem there are two possible reactions: there are those who say, "let us create social institutions which will make large-scale war impossible"; there are others who say, "let us not allow war to become too scientific. We cannot perhaps go back to bows and arrows, but let us at any rate agree with our enemies that, if we fight them, both sides will fight inefficiently." For my part, I favour the former answer, since I cannot see that either side could be expected to observe an agreement not to use modern weapons if once war had broken out. It is on this ground that I do not think that there will long continue to be human beings unless methods are found of permanently preventing large-scale wars. But this is a serious question as to which I will say no more at the moment. I shall return to it presently.

The substitution of machines for human labour raises problems which are likely to become acute in the not very distant future. These problems are not new. They began with the Industrial Revolution, which ruined large numbers of skilled and industrious handicraftsmen, inflicting upon them hardships that they had in no way deserved and that they bitterly resented. But their troubles were transitory: they died; and such of their children as survived sought other occupations.

The sufferers had no political power and were not able to offer any effective resistance to "progress." Nowadays, in democratic countries, the political situation is different and wage earners cannot be expected to submit **tamely** to starvation. But if we are to believe **Norbert Wiener**'s book on **cybernetics**—and I see no reason why we should not—it should soon be possible to keep up the existing level of production with a very much smaller number of workers. The more economical methods, one may suppose, would be introduced during a war while the workers were at the front, if such a war were not quickly ended by H-bomb extermination, and when the survivors returned their former jobs would no longer be available. The social discontent resulting from such a situation would be very grave. It could be dealt with in a **totalitarian** country, but a democracy could

exterminate 消灭

Norbert Wiener 诺伯特·维纳（1894—1964），美国数学家和哲学家，控制论的创始人，曾为麻省理工学院教授。

tamely 温顺地，驯服地

cybernetics 控制论

totalitarian 极权主义的

only deal with it by radical changes in its social philosophy and even in its ethics. Work has been thought to be a duty, but in such a situation there would be little work to do and duty would have to take new forms.

Changes in political philosophy are necessary for several reasons. One of the most important is that modern techniques make society more organic in the sense that its parts are more interdependent and an injury to one individual or group is more likely than it formerly was to cause injury to other individuals or groups. It is easier to kill a man than to kill a **sponge** because he is more highly organized and more centralized. In like manner it is easier to inflict vital damage upon a scientific community than upon a community of nomads or scattered peasants. This increase of interdependence makes it necessary to limit freedom in various ways which liberals in the past considered undesirable. There are two spheres in which such limitation is especially necessary: the one is in economics; and the other, in the relations between states.

Take economics first. Suppose, as is not improbable, that most of the power used in industry comes to be distributed from a fairly small number of atomic power-stations, and suppose that the men working in these stations retained the right to strike. They could completely **paralyze** the industrial life of a nation and could **levy** almost unlimited **blackmail** in the form of demands for higher wages. No community would tolerate such a state of affairs. The workers in power-stations would have to have **understudies** like actors in a theatre, and the forces of the state would have to be employed if necessary to enable the understudies to replace workers on strike. Another example, which war has already brought to the fore, is the supply and use of raw materials. Whenever raw materials are scarce their distribution has to be controlled and not left to the free play of **unfettered** economic forces.

Scarcity of this sort has hitherto been thought of as a transitory phenomenon due to the needs and **ravages** of war. But it is likely to remain, in regard to many essentials, a normal condition of highly developed industry. Some central authority for the allocation of raw

sponge 海绵

paralyze 使瘫痪
levy 召集；索取
blackmail 勒索

understudy 候补演员

unfettered 无拘无束的

ravage 毁坏

materials must therefore be expected as a necessary limitation of economic freedom. Another unavoidable limitation comes from the vastness of some obviously desirable enterprises. To bring fertility to the interior of Australia and to parts of Siberia is almost certainly possible, but only by an expenditure far beyond the capacity of private enterprise. One may expect that the progress of science will increase the number of such possible enterprises. Perhaps it will be possible in time to make the Sahara rainy, or even to make northern Canada warm. But, if such things become possible, they will be possible only for whole communities and not for private corporations.

Even more important than the limitations of economic liberty are the limitations on the liberty of states. The liberal doctrine of nationality, which was preached by liberals before 1848 and embodied in the ***Treaty of Versailles*** by President Wilson, had its justification as a protest against alien domination. But to allow complete liberty to any national state is just as **anarchic** as it would be to allow complete liberty to an individual. There are things which an individual must not do because the criminal law forbids them. The law and the police are in most cases strong enough to prevent such things from being done: murderers are a very small percentage of the population of any civilized country. But the relations between states are not governed by law and cannot be until there is a supranational armed force strong enough to enforce the decisions of a supranational authority. In the past, although the wars resulting from international anarchy caused much suffering and destruction, mankind was able to survive them, and, on the whole, the risks of war were thought less **irksome** than the controls that would be necessary to prevent it. This is ceasing to be true. The risks of war have become so great that the continued existence of our species either has become or soon will become incompatible with the new methods of scientific destruction.

The new dangers resulting from our more organic society call for certain changes in the kind of character that is admired. The bold **buccaneer**, or the great conqueror such as Alexander or Napoleon, has been admired and is still admired although the world can no longer afford this type of character. We come here upon a difficulty. It is a good thing that people should be adventurous and that there

---

Treaty of Versailles 《凡尔赛条约》，第一次世界大战后战胜国（协约国）对战败国（同盟国）的和约，其主要目的是削弱德国的势力。

anarchic 无政府（主义）的

irksome 使人烦恼的

buccaneer 投机取巧者

should be scope for individual enterprise; but the adventure and enterprise, if they are not to bring total disaster, must steer clear of certain fields in which they were formerly possible. You may still, without harm to your fellow men, wish to be the first man to reach the moon. You may wish to be a great poet or a great composer or a man who advances the boundaries of scientific knowledge. Such adventure injures no one. But if Napoleon is your ideal, you must be restrained. Certain kinds of anarchic self-assertion, which are splendid in the literature of tragedy, have come to involve too much risk. A motorist alone on an empty road may drive as he pleases, but in crowded traffic he must obey the rules. More and more the lives of individuals come to resemble the motorist in traffic rather than the lonely driver in an empty desert.

I come at last to a question which is causing considerable concern and **perplexity** to many men of science, namely: what is their social duty toward this new world that they have been creating? I do not think this question is easy or simple. The pure man of science, as such, is concerned with the advancement of knowledge, and in his professional moments he takes it for granted that the advancement of knowledge is desirable. But inevitably he finds himself **casting his pearls before swine**. Men who do not understand his scientific work can utilize the knowledge that he provides. The new techniques to which it gives rise often have totally unexpected effects. The men who decide what use shall be made of the new techniques are not necessarily possessed of any exceptional degree of wisdom. They are mainly politicians whose professional skill consists in knowing how to play upon the emotions of masses of men. The emotions which easily **sway** masses are very seldom the best of which the individuals composing the masses are capable. And so the scientist finds that he has unintentionally placed new powers in the hands of **reckless** men. He may easily come to doubt, in moments of depression or overwork, whether the world would not be a happier place if science did not exist. He knows that science gives power and that the power which it gives could be used to increase human welfare; but he knows also that very often it is used, not so, but in the very opposite direction. Is he on this account to view himself as an unintentional **malefactor**?

perplexity 困惑

casting pearls before swine 对牛弹琴

sway 使动摇

reckless 不计后果的

malefactor 作恶的人

I do not think so. I think we must retain the belief that scientific knowledge is one of the glories of man. I will not maintain that knowledge can never do harm. I think such general **propositions** can almost always be refuted by well-chosen examples. What I will maintain—and maintain vigorously—is that knowledge is very much more often useful than harmful and that fear of knowledge is very much more often harmful than useful. Suppose you are a scientific pioneer and you make some discovery of great scientific importance, and suppose you say to yourself, "I am afraid this discovery will do harm": you know that other people are likely to make the same discovery if they are allowed suitable opportunities for research; you must therefore, if you do not wish the discovery to become public, either discourage your sort of research or control publication by a board of censors. Nine times out of ten, the board of **censors** will object to knowledge that is in fact useful—e.g., knowledge concerning **contraceptives**—rather than to knowledge that would in fact be harmful. It is very difficult to foresee the social effects of new knowledge, and it is very easy from the sheer force of habit to shrink from new knowledge such as might promote new kinds of behaviour.

(2,905 words)

proposition 命题

censor 审查员

contraceptive 避孕措施

 Recall

Answer the following questions with the information from the passage.

1. In the case of man and science, what is the unique factor that is changing the world?
2. Which is more challenging for scientists, grappling with the science that deals with man, or persuading the world to listen to what they have discovered?
3. What does Russell state is an obvious problem raised by a scientific technique?
4. What is the possible drawback for some governments taking steps to prevent the denudation of the soil?
5. What does the author think of scientific knowledge?

II Interpret

Answer the following questions by analysing the passage.

6. In Paragraph 3, the author says "The question of raw materials is more difficult and complex than the question of food." In what way is the question of raw materials more difficult and complex? How could the use of raw materials be "conservative" (in Paragraph 4)?

7. The author calls for changes in political philosophy in Paragraph 9. Why are changes in political philosophy necessary? How does the author illustrate the limitations that are needed in this article?

III Evaluate & Connect

Answer the following question by relating the passage to your own experience.

8. What do you think is scientists' social duty toward this new world they have been creating? Do you think they are responsible for the potential negative consequences of their new creation?

Unit 2

Science Literacy

Synopsis

习近平总书记指出:"科技创新、科学普及是实现创新发展的两翼,要把科学普及放在与科技创新同等重要的位置。"科学普及的前提需要回答"什么是科学素养,其重要性如何及其缺失的缘由"。但是,对于非科学专业的大学生来说,充斥着各种方程式的科学课堂无疑让他们望而却步。在 Text A 中,Robert Pool 讲述的通识教育项目一改古板的科学课堂,设情境、提问题、探究竟,使得大学科学课堂妙趣横生;Text B 将科学素养置于运用科学进行社会生活的视角下讨论,从美学和知识关联的角度阐述其重要性,并提出了提高科学素养的基本原则。

Warm-up

Official surveys in China have shown steady increase of the proportion of scientifically literate Chinese citizens. As the following bar graph shows, the proportion was 6.20%, 10.56%, 14.14% respectively for the years 2015, 2020 and 2023.

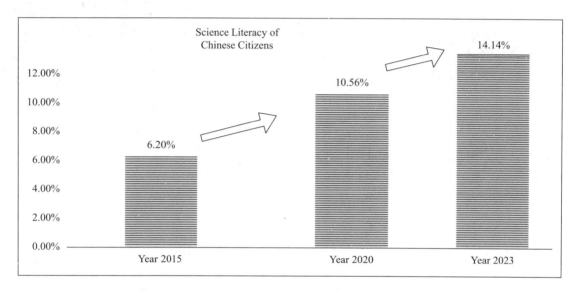

Are you scientifically literate? What level of scientific literacy is necessary for responsible participation in our society and for leading a rewarding professional life and personal life? Rate the importance of each of the following capabilities of scientifically literate people.

Scientific Literacy Survey

Statements of Capabilities	Not necessary Essential 1 ⟷ 5				
Pose a question that can be addressed by the scientific method, e.g., state a hypothesis.	1	2	3	4	5
Provide a scientific explanation for a natural process, e.g., photosynthesis, digestion and combustion.	1	2	3	4	5
Assess the appropriateness of the methodology of an experiment.	1	2	3	4	5
Read and understand articles on science in a newspaper.	1	2	3	4	5
Read and interpret graphs displaying scientific information.	1	2	3	4	5

(Continued)

Statements of Capabilities	Not necessary Essential 1 ⟵⟶ 5
Believe that scientific knowledge is worth pursuing even if it never yields practical benefits.	1 2 3 4 5
Define basic scientific terms, e.g., DNA, molecule and electricity.	1 2 3 4 5
Design an experiment that is a valid test of a hypothesis.	1 2 3 4 5
Engage in a scientifically informed discussion of a contemporary issue, e.g., the germ theory of disease.	1 2 3 4 5
Be inclined to challenge authority on evidence that supports scientific statements.	1 2 3 4 5
Describe natural phenomenon, e.g., the phases of the moon.	1 2 3 4 5
Apply scientific information in personal decision making, e.g., ozone depletion and the use of aerosols.	1 2 3 4 5
Locate valid scientific information when needed.	1 2 3 4 5

Adapted from Audrey B. Champagne (1989) in *Educational Leadership*

From the list of statements above, which five do you think are the most important characteristics of a scientifically literate person? Why?

Text A

Background information

This article was published in the journal *Science* in 1990. The author, Dr. Robert Pool, is a world-renowned author, consultant, and speaker. He has worked as a writer and editor at the world's two most prestigious science publications—*Science* and *Nature*. The most common methods of teaching chemistry are lectures, demonstrations and laboratory activities. It is very important for chemistry teachers to foster students' skills in critical thinking, deductive reasoning, problem-solving and communication. However, not all students like learning chemistry, so an overarching goal for chemistry teachers is to involve those uninterested students by making chemistry more relevant to their life.

Freshman Chemistry Was Never Like This

Robert Pool

To battle science illiteracy among college students, the New Liberal Arts program tries a fresh approach to teaching science.

Larry Kaplan's chemistry lab was just getting under way when a campus security officer rushed in and announced there had been a hit-and-run accident behind the chemistry building. "Hold on," Kaplan told his students, "Class isn't over yet. Bring your notebooks and follow me to the crime scene." It didn't take long for the class to figure out that the "accident" was a **fake**, but everyone played along. They called an ambulance for the "victim" (Kaplan's daughter), **roped off** the scene of the accident, and began collecting evidence. Their assignment: to identify the vehicle that supposedly hit the girl by comparing glass **fragments** found at the scene with glass samples taken from the headlights of the suspect's vehicle.

This is obviously not Chem 101 with test tubes and **balances** and smelly chemicals. And that's precisely the point. Kaplan, chairman of the chemistry department at Williams College in Williamstown,

fake 虚假的事

rope off 用绳子围起来

fragment 碎片

balance 天平

Massachusetts, is one of a new **breed** of science teachers who are trying innovative curricula and novel classroom techniques to reach students who would otherwise never learn much science.

Science courses for non-majors aren't new, of course. They've been around for decades in such classes as "physics for poets." But since 1983, when the Department of Education published "A Nation at Risk," warning of the "rising tide of **mediocrity**" in our schools, there has been a growing consensus that something **drastic** needs to be done to improve the science literacy of U.S. students. Now nearly every college and university can point to one or a few Larry Kaplans on its faculty, but most of the efforts have been scattered, performed by imaginative teachers working alone. One coordinated, multi-college project, however, has been quietly **chipping away at** the problem since 1982—the year before the education department brought it to the nation's attention.

The New Liberal Arts, a program funded by the Albert P. Sloan Foundation of New York City, has spent more than $20 million at three dozen liberal arts colleges to develop new ways to teach science to nonscience students. The results include Kaplan's chemistry course and more than 200 others, covering the **gamut** of disciplines from engineering to the physical, biological, and social sciences. And two weeks ago, 80 participants gathered at Trinity College in Hartford, Connecticut, to discuss their successes and failures in the NLA program. The lessons they have learned may well prove valuable to many other schools struggling to turn back the rising tide.

Kaplan's chemistry lab illustrates one of the basic themes that emerged from the NLA workshop: Science must be taught in a way that will catch the interest of the student. **Esoteric** vocabulary and **mind-boggling** formulas, no matter how essential they may seem to practitioners, will only scare away the liberal arts student who is already suspicious of science.

Kaplan **draws** his students **in** by talking about **forensics**. He discusses the **admissibility** of evidence, the importance of collecting appropriate controls, and how to analyse a crime scene. "All during this time, the students think they're not doing any chemistry," he says. "But what I'm really doing is teaching them about the scientific

---

breed 类型

mediocrity 平庸之人
drastic 激烈的

chip away at 逐渐缓解

gamut 全范围

esoteric 深奥的
mind-boggling 难以理解的；伤脑筋的

draw in 使参与
forensics 取证；法医学
admissibility 证据的可采纳性

method, the importance of clearly identified samples, the use of controls and standards, and other aspects of doing good science."

And they get hands-on experience in the lab. They analyse the glass samples from the hit-and-run accident by measuring their density and **refractive indices**. In another session, they drink measured amounts of beer and correlate their **breathalyser** readings with their alcohol consumption. The lab also includes plenty of the more traditional chemical analysis techniques, Kaplan says, but the experiments are always prompted by something from forensic science.

"The central theme [of the New Liberal Arts program] is the use of modern technology as a vehicle for motivating students and guiding them," says John Truxal of the State University of New York at Stony Brook, who is co-director of the NLA. This distinguishes the NLA curriculum from most of the traditional science-for-non-scientists courses. "Such courses are usually non-mathematical, **watered-down** versions of the normal introductory courses," Truxal points out, and as such they are poorly designed to promote scientific literacy. Introductory courses may give majors everything they need to continue on to more advanced classes, but a student who is only going to take one physics (or chemistry or biology or geology) course needs both much less and much more.

A nonscience student can actually be shown much more science in a single course than a science major since the non-major does not need all the groundwork for later courses, says physicist Ralph Baierlein at Wesleyan University in Middletown, Connecticut. Baierlein teaches a course called "Newton to Einstein: The Trail of Light." Students are fascinated, he says, by such concepts as wave-particle **duality** and special relativity, which they would not come across until they were upperclassmen if they majored in physics. That fascination has made the course popular, Baierlein says. Expecting 20 to 30 students the first time he offered it, he got 141. The next year, 170 students signed up, including about 20% science and math majors.

To **get** the concepts **across** without equations and technical explanations, Baierlein gives plenty of classroom demonstrations. "It

---

refractive index 折射率

breathalyser 呼吸分析仪

watered-down 淡化的；弱化的

duality 二象性（此处特指光的波粒二象性）；二元性

get across 使被理解

enables people to see things, to believe things," he explains. In one of his favourites, he holds a **neon**-filled tube in an electromagnetic field to show how excited atoms **emit** light. "That is so striking a demonstration that a picture of it actually showed up last year on the university calendar," he says.

A second physics-for-nonmajors course at Wesleyan, "The **Quantum** World," has proved less successful, Baierlein says. The concepts from quantum mechanics fascinate the students, he says, but are too far above their heads. "It's like watching *Star Trek*—It's fun, but I don't know how much they're learning." The **moral**: "You can't teach abstract **algebra** to fourth-grade kids. Some things just can't be done because the mind isn't ready for them."

Several teachers at the Trinity College meeting described making scientific concepts more understandable to students with the imaginative use of some common high-tech devices. Physicist **Theodore Ducas** at Wellesley College in Wellesley, Massachusetts, for instance, has **harnessed** the video camera to help students understand **dynamics** and the laws of motion. In one experiment, a student **tosses** an object in the air while another student films it, holding the camera steady. The students then run the film **frame** by frame and measure the position of the object as a **function** of time, which is given by the camera's frame rate. They can see for themselves that masses in a gravitational field really do move in a **parabola**, Ducas says, and also that their horizontal velocity remains constant throughout the motion.

In a more **whimsical** demonstration, Ducas travelled in an elevator up and down 40 floors of Boston's **John Hancock Building**, standing on a scale and pointing a video camera at the readout between his feet. Playing the video-tape to his class, he showed the students how to calculate the acceleration of the elevator based on the change in his weight, and with this to compute the elevator's speed and position.

"Half of the introductory physics labs at Wellesley, both for science and nonscience majors, are now based on AVID [Active Video Instructional Development]," Ducas says, and next he plans to extend the technique to teaching **calculus**.

Although the NLA courses do not emphasize solving equations, they do place a great deal of weight on developing "quantitative reasoning"—the ability to think in numerical terms and to make decisions involving probabilities and approximations. For example, Ducas confronts his students with the question of whether to perform **amniocentesis** on a **foetus** that might have **Down syndrome**. Since the procedure slightly increases risk of **miscarriage**, the decision involves weighing various probabilities—how likely it is that the foetus carries the **chromosomal** abnormality for Down's syndrome versus the chance of amniocentesis causing a miscarriage, for example. "Our fundamental obligation is to teach students the skills to handle options," Ducas says. "This means that the students must, first, learn how to understand options and, second, develop skills in decision-making."

After eight years of experience, the New Liberal Arts program is ready to share what it has learned with other colleges and universities, says Samuel Goldberg, NLA's program officer at the Sloan Foundation. Participants have published three textbooks based on NLA courses, with another nine planned. The foundation is also making available about 25 **monographs** on individual topics that can be integrated into existing courses and 25 extended syllabi for teachers who would like to pattern classes after some of the successful NLA programs. Interested faculty members can get copies free from Truxal at Stony Brook.

Unfortunately for the NLA, funding from the Sloan Foundation is coming to a close—the program will end in 1991. One of the topics at the Trinity meeting was where the money will come from to continue work on teaching science to nonscience students. Duncan McBride, a program director in the division of undergraduate science, engineering, and mathematics education at the National Science Foundation, says the NSF might fund some of it, especially cooperative efforts that involve teachers from a number of institutions. Although the NLA has developed some good courses, McBride says, a key question is whether other teachers at other institutions can adapt the material to their own settings. In addition to the NSF, Truxal suggests **soliciting** businesses for support: "I think corporate America

amniocentesis 羊膜穿刺术	
foetus 胎儿	
Down syndrome 唐氏综合征	
miscarriage 流产	
chromosomal 染色体的	
monograph 专著	
solicit 征求	

has a tremendous stake in education, and we haven't even touched that resource."

May the force be with you. Teacher Ralph Baierlein combats science illiteracy not with laser swords but with a demonstration of gas-filled tubes that glow in an electric field.

Teaching science appreciation

"This course is likely to be different from any science course you've had before," Robert Hazen told his students on the first day of class. "Most people aren't going to be scientists, and what we're trying to do instead of making you scientists is to make you people who can appreciate science." Drawing analogies with art and music appreciation courses and with sports, Hazen said, "Science appreciation is a lot like a sporting event. You don't have to be able to **slam dunk** to appreciate Magic Johnson."

Hazen's course, developed with colleague James Trefil at George Mason University in Fairfax, Virginia, **revolves** around "The Great Ideas in Science." It contrasts with the New Liberal Arts program, whose courses focus on specific, limited topics and use technology to draw students in. But both programs aim to combat the problem of science illiteracy among college nonscience majors. "The students

slam dunk 强力灌篮

revolve 环绕；围绕

we get come into the course both scared of science and unable to comprehend even the simplest newspaper article about science," says Hazen, who also works as a geophysicist at the Carnegie Institution of Washington. Now, after the semesters of teaching the course, Hazen and Trefil believe their approach is working.

The theme of the course is simple, Hazen says: "A small number of laws or concepts make up an **overarching** framework for everything that every scientist does." He and Trefil offer 18 of these great ideas, including "Everything is made of atoms," "The universe was born in a giant explosion and has been expanding ever since," "All living things are made from cells, the chemical factories of life," and "All life evolved by natural selection." Each concept is accompanied by specific examples that the students can relate to. When teaching about energy, for instance, Hazen and Trefil might discuss the moral and practical implications of using nuclear power.

Along with the great ideas of science, the two scientists also teach about the process of doing science—observation, forming hypotheses, and testing theories. Nor do they forget the personal side of science. In explaining the **stereotypes** of scientists, for instance, Hazen joked to his class that physicists are generally pictured with **scruffy** beards and T-shirts, chemists as wearing suits ("because they're all consulting for chemical companies"), and geologists are seen in **flannel** shirts and hiking boots. "The students come out with an understanding that science is a human process and that it deals with how the physical universe behaves."

Judging from student response, Hazen and Trefil have found a successful formula for teaching science to nonscience majors. Students at George Mason fill out detailed evaluations, and "they've been quite flattering," Hazen says. "Quite a number of students have said it's the best course they've ever had." Even more encouraging, he adds that "I've had students come up to me a year later and say that now they read the science section in newspapers." They probably still read the sports section first, but at least a few students have learned to appreciate science.

---

overarching 总体的，包罗万象的

stereotype 刻板印象

scruffy 邋遢的

flannel 法兰绒

Unit 2 Science Literacy

❶ Recall

Answer the following questions with the information from the passage.

1. What is a typical Chem 101 classroom like?
2. What does Kaplan's chemistry lab illustrate about science teaching?
3. According to Baierlein, why has "The Quantum World" proved less successful?
4. What is quantitative reasoning as emphasized by the NLA courses?

❷ Interpret

Answer the following questions by analysing the passage.

5. In Paragraph 4, the author says, "The lessons they have learned may well prove valuable to many other schools struggling to turn back the rising tide." What does "the rising tide" refer to?
6. In Paragraph 8, the author says, "a student who is only going to take one physics (or chemistry or biology or geology) course needs both much less and much more." What does the student need less and more of?
7. How is Robert Hazen's course different from Larry Kaplan's chemistry class?

❸ Evaluate & Connect

Answer the following question by relating the passage to your own experience.

8. If you were a science teacher, what teaching approaches would you take for nonscience students, especially for those who are suspicious of science?

Text B

Background information

The text is extracted from *Science Matters: Achieving Scientific Literacy* published by Anchor in 2009. It is a science book that appeals to the general readers. It is authored by Robert M. Hazen and James Trefil. Professor Hazen and Professor Trefil are both prolific award-winning authors and are fellows of the American Association for the Advancement of Science. Hazen's recent research focuses on the possible role of minerals in the origin of life, mineral evolution, and the coevolution of the geosphere and biosphere. Trefil is known for his writing and interest in teaching science to non-scientists. Hazen and Trefil also co-authored *The Sciences: An Integrated Approach*, a popular textbook that focuses on helping students to achieve scientific literacy.

Scientific Literacy: What It Is, Why It's Important, and Why We don't Have It

Robert M. Hazen   James Trefil

Some time in the next few days you are going to pick up your newspaper and see a headline like "Major Advance in Stem Cells Reported" or "New Theory of Global Warming Proposed." The stories following these headlines will be important. They will deal with issues that directly affect your life—issues about which you, as a citizen, will have to form an opinion if you are to take part in our country's political discourse. More than ever before, scientific and technological issues dominate, from global climate change, to the teaching of evolution, to the perceived gradual decline of American competitiveness. Being able to understand these debates is becoming as important to you as being able to read. You must be scientifically literate.

In spite of decades of **well-meaning** efforts, scientists and educators have failed to provide many Americans with the fundamental

well-meaning 善意的

background knowledge we all need to cope with the complex scientific and technological world of today and tomorrow. The aim of this book is to allow you to acquire that background—to fill in whatever blanks may have been left by your formal education. Our aim, in short, is to give you the information you need to become scientifically literate.

What is scientific literacy?

For us, scientific literacy **constitutes** the knowledge you need to understand public issues. It is a mix of facts, vocabulary, concepts, history, and philosophy. It is not the specialized stuff of the experts, but the more general, less precise knowledge used in political discourse. If you can understand the news of the day as it relates to science, if you can take articles with headlines about stem cell research and the greenhouse effect and put them in a meaningful context—in short, if you can treat news about science in the same way that you treat everything else that comes over your horizon, then as far as we are concerned you are scientifically literate.

constitute 构成、构筑

This definition of scientific literacy is going to seem rather **minimal**, perhaps even totally inadequate, to some scholars. We feel very strongly that those who insist that everyone must understand science at a deep level are confusing two important but separate aspects of scientific knowledge. The fact of the matter is that doing science is clearly distinct from using science; scientific literacy concerns only the latter.

minimal 最小的

There is no need for the average citizen to be able to do what scientists do. You don't have to know how to design a **microchip** or **sequence** a section of DNA to understand the daily news, any more than you have to be able to design an airplane in order to understand how it can fly.

microchip 微芯片
sequence 排序

But the fact that you don't have to know how to design an airplane doesn't change the fact that you live in a world where airplanes exist, and your world is different because of them. In the same way, advances in fields like **nanotechnology** and bioengineering will affect your life in many ways, and you need to have enough background knowledge to understand how these changes are likely to

nanotechnology 纳米技术

occur and what their consequences are likely to be for you and your children. You must be able to put new advances into a context that will allow you to take part in the national debate about them.

Like cultural literacy, scientific literacy does not refer to detailed, specialized knowledge—the sort of things an expert would know. When you come across a term like **"superconductor"** in a newspaper article, it is enough to know that it refers to a material that conducts electricity without loss, that the main **impediment** to the widespread use of superconductors is that they operate only at very low temperatures, and that finding ways to remove this impediment is a major research goal in materials science today. You can be scientifically literate without knowing how a superconductor works at the atomic level, what the various species of superconductor are, or how one could go about **fabricating** a superconducting material.

Intense study of a particular field of science does not necessarily make one scientifically literate. Indeed, it has been our experience that working scientists are often illiterate outside their own field of professional expertise. For example, when we asked a group of two dozen physicists and geologists to explain to us the difference between DNA and RNA, a basic piece of information in the life sciences, we found only three who could do so, and all three of those did research in areas where this knowledge was useful. And although we haven't done an **equivalent** test on biologists—by asking them, for example, to explain the difference between a superconductor and a semiconductor—there is no doubt in our minds that we would find the same sort of discouraging result if we did. The fact of the matter is that the education of professional scientists is often just as narrowly focused as the education of any other group of professionals, and scientists are just as likely to be ignorant of scientific matters as anyone else. You should keep this in mind the next time a Nobel **laureate** speaks **ex cathedra** on issues outside his or her own field of specialization.

Finally, one aspect of knowledge is sometimes **lumped** into scientific literacy but is actually quite different. You sometimes see discussions of scientific literacy **couched** in terms of statements like "The average new employee has no idea how to use a BlackBerry"

superconductor 超导体	
impediment 障碍	
fabricate 制造	
equivalent 等同的	
laureate 荣誉获得者	
ex cathedra 拉丁语，"出于权威"	
lump 把……归并一起	
couch（用某种文体或方式）表达	

or "The average American is dependent on technology but can't even program a DVR to record when no one's home." These statements are probably true, and they undoubtedly reflect an unhappy state of affairs in American society. We would prefer, however, to talk of them in terms of technological rather than scientific literacy.

The scope of the problem

The effectiveness of American science education has changed little since the 1987 commencement of Harvard University, when a filmmaker carried a camera into the crowd of **gowned** graduates and, at random, posed a simple question: "Why is it hotter in summer than in winter?" The results, displayed graphically in the film *A Private Universe*, were that only two of the twenty-three students **queried** could answer the question correctly. Even **allowing for** the **festive** atmosphere of a graduation ceremony, this result reveals the failure of America's most prestigious universities to turn out students who are in command of **rudimentary** facts about the physical world. An informal survey taken at our own university—where one can argue that teaching undergraduates enjoys a higher status than at some other institutions—shows results that are scarcely more encouraging. Fully half of the seniors who filled out our scientific literacy survey could not correctly answer the question "What is the difference between an atom and a molecule?"

These results are not minor **blemishes** on a sea of **otherwise** faultless academic performances. Every university in the country has the same dirty little secret: we are all turning out scientific illiterates, students incapable of understanding many of the important newspaper items published on the very day of their graduation.

The problem, of course, is not limited to universities. We hear over and over again about how poorly American high school and middle school students **fare** when compared to students in other developed countries on standardized tests. Scholars who make it their business to study such things estimate that fewer than 7% of American adults can be classed as scientifically literate. Even among college graduates (22%) and those with graduate degrees (26%), the number of Americans who are scientifically literate by the standards

gowned 穿着礼服的

query 询问
allow for 考虑到
festive 喜庆的

rudimentary 基本的

blemish 瑕疵
otherwise 在其他各方面的

fare 成功

of these studies (which tend to be somewhat less demanding than our own) is not very high.

The numbers, then, tell the same story as the **anecdotes**. Americans as a whole simply have not been exposed to science sufficiently or in a way that communicates, the knowledge they need to have to cope with the life they will have to lead in the twenty-first century.

Why scientific literacy is important

Why be scientifically literate? A number of different arguments can be made to convince you it's important. Here we list two of them:

➢ the argument from **aesthetics**

➢ the argument from intellectual connectedness

The argument from aesthetics is somewhat **amorphous**, and **is closely allied to** arguments that are usually made to support liberal education in general. It goes like this: We live in a world that operates according to a few general laws of nature. Everything you do from the moment you get up to the moment you go to bed happens because of the working of one of these laws. This exceedingly beautiful and elegant view of the world is the **crowning** achievement of centuries of work by scientists. There is intellectual and aesthetic satisfaction to be gained from seeing the unity between a pot of water on a stove and the slow march of the continents, between the colours of the rainbow and the behaviour of the fundamental constituents of matter. The scientifically illiterate person has been cut off from an enriching part of life, just as surely as a person who cannot read.

Secondly, we come to the argument of intellectual coherence. It has become a commonplace to note that scientific findings often play a crucial role in setting the intellectual climate of an era. Copernicus's discovery of the heliocentric universe played an important role in sweeping away the old thinking of the Middle Ages and **ushering in** the Age of **Enlightenment**. Darwin's discovery of the principle of natural selection made the world seem less planned, less directed than it had been before; and in the twentieth century the work of Freud and the development of quantum mechanics made it seem (at least superficially) less rational. In all of these cases, the general intellectual **tenor** of the times—what Germans call the **zeitgeist**—

was influenced by developments in science. How, the argument goes, can anyone hope to appreciate the deep underlying threads of intellectual life in his or her own time without understanding the science that goes with it?

What to do

The beginning of a solution to America's problem with scientific literacy, both for those still in school and those whose formal education has been completed, lies in a simple statement:

If you expect someone to know something, you have to tell him or her what it is.

This principle is so obvious that it scarcely needs defending (although you'd be amazed at how often it is ignored within the halls of **academe**). It's obvious that if we want people to be able to understand issues involving genetic engineering, then we have to tell them what genetic engineering is, how DNA and RNA work, and how all living systems use the same genetic code. If we expect people to come to an intelligent decision on whether tens of billions of tax dollars should be spent on alternatives to fossil fuels—development of biofuels, new nuclear power plants, **wind turbines**, and the like—then we have to tell them about the nature of energy in general and the potential benefits and risks associated with each specific energy source.

academe 学术界

wind turbine
风电机组；风力涡轮机

But this argument, as simple as it seems, runs **counter** to powerful institutional forces in the scientific community, particularly the academic community. To function as a citizen, you need to know a little bit about a lot of different sciences—a little biology, a little geology, a little physics, and so on. But universities (and, by extension, primary and secondary schools) are set up to teach one science at a time. Thus, a fundamental mismatch exists between the kinds of knowledge educational institutions are equipped to impart and the kind of knowledge the citizen needs.

counter 冲突地，对抗地

So scientists must define what parts of our craft are essential for the scientifically literate citizen and then put that knowledge together in a coherent package. For those still in school, this package can be delivered in new courses of study. For the great majority of

Americans—those whom the educational system has already failed—this information has to be made available in other forms.

Science is organized around certain central concepts, certain **pillars** that support the entire structure. There are a limited number of such concepts (or "laws"), but they account for everything we see in the world around us. Since there are an infinite number of phenomena and only a few laws, the logical structure of science is **analogous** to a spider's web. Start anywhere on the web and work inward, and eventually you come to the same core. Understanding this core of knowledge, then, is what science is all about.

	pillar 支柱
	analogous 相似的

I Recall

Answer the following questions with the information from the passage.

1. What is the minimal definition of scientific literacy that the authors provided?
2. What should a scientifically literate person know about a term like "superconductor" from a newspaper?
3. In what ways is scientific literacy important?
4. What can be done to eliminate Americans' scientific illiteracy?

II Interpret

Answer the following questions by analysing the passage.

5. Are working scientists scientifically literate outside their field of science? What is the implication for this on science literacy?
6. Is science illiteracy a serious problem in the U.S.?

III Evaluate & Connect

Answer the following questions by relating the passage to your own experience.

7. Which of the following is a valid scientific argument? What does it reveal about science literacy?

> A. Measurements of sea level on the Gulf Coast taken this year are lower than normal; the average monthly measurements were almost 0.1cm lower than normal in some areas. These facts prove that rising sea levels are not a problem.

B. A strain of mice was genetically engineered to lack a certain gene, and the mice were unable to reproduce. Introduction of the gene back into the mutant mice restored their ability to reproduce. These facts indicate that the gene is essential for mouse reproduction.

C. A poll revealed that 34% of Americans believe that dinosaurs and early humans co-existed because fossil footprints of each species were found in the same location. This widespread belief is appropriate evidence to support the claim that humans did not evolve from ape ancestors.

D. This winter, the northeastern U.S. received record amounts of snowfall, and the average monthly temperatures were more than 2°F lower than normal in some areas. These facts indicate that climate change is occurring.

Adapted from *Test of Scientific Literacy Skills* by Washburn University

8. *The Outline of the Action Plan for National Scientific Literacy (2021—2035)* (《全民科学素质行动规划纲要（2021—2035）》) stipulates that by 2025, over 25% of Chinese citizens should be scientifically literate, while by 2035, it should exceed 35%. What measures do you think can be taken to improve science literacy for people of different age groups?

Chemical Science

Synopsis

  什么是化学？化学是科学的一个分支，涉及元素和化合物的属性、组成和结构，元素和化合物如何变化，以及它们变化时释放或吸收的能量。本单元将带领读者走进化学的奇妙世界，这里不仅有原子和元素，还有著名的化学家。Text A 主要介绍了 17 世纪和 18 世纪原子理论的发展以及对此做出重要贡献的几位化学家；Text B 介绍了极端低温条件下的化学探索和应用。

Warm-up

Below are brief introductions to some famous chemists. Are you familiar with them? Choose one and share what else you know about them with your partners.

Dmitri Mendeleev
Born: February 8, 1834
Died: February 2, 1907

Russian chemist Dmitri Mendeleev created the Periodic Law and the version of the Periodic Table of Elements that revolutionized the field of chemistry.

Rosalind Franklin
Born: July 25, 1920
Died: April 16, 1958

Chemist and X-ray crystallographer Rosalind Franklin is remembered for her groundbreaking X-ray diffraction studies of DNA, which played a role in the Nobel Prize-winning discovery of the double helix structure of DNA by Francis Crick, James Watson, and Maurice Wilkins later.

Antoine Lavoisier
Born: August 26, 1743
Died: May 8, 1794

Antoine Lavoisier was a French chemist and nobleman. Widely regarded as the father of modern chemistry, Lavoisier had a major influence on the history of chemistry as well as biology. He also helped devise the metric system.

Tu Youyou
Born: December 30, 1930

Chinese phytochemist and malariologist Tu Youyou is best remembered for her Nobel Prize-winning discovery of the anti-malarial drug *qinghaosu* (青蒿素), or artemisinin. She is the first Chinese female Nobel laureate. A tuberculosis infection in her youth inspired her to step into medicine.

Text A

Background information

This article is extracted from *A Little History of Science* published by Yale University Press in 2012. The book was authored by William Bynum, emeritus professor at the Wellcome Trust Centre for the History of Medicine, University College London. This inviting book tells a great adventure story: the history of science. It takes readers to the stars through the telescope, as the sun replaces the Earth at the centre of our universe. It delves beneath the surface of the planet, charts the evolution of chemistry's periodic table, and introduces the physics that explain electricity, gravity, and the structure of atoms. It recounts the scientific quest that revealed the DNA molecule and opened up unimagined new vistas for exploration. Emphasizing surprising and personal stories of scientists both famous and unsung, *A Little History of Science* traces the march of science through the centuries.

Tiny Pieces of Matter

William Bynum

Atoms used to have a pretty bad name. Remember the ancient Greeks with their notion of atoms as part of a universe that was random and without purpose? So how is it that for us today, being made up of atoms seems so natural?

The modern "atom" was the **brainchild** of a thoroughly respectable **Quaker**, **John Dalton** (1766—1844). A weaver's son, he went to a good school near where he was born, in the English Lake District. He was especially skilled in mathematics and science, and a famous blind mathematician encouraged his scientific ambitions. Dalton settled in nearby Manchester, a thriving and rapidly growing town during the early Industrial Revolution, when factories began to dominate the making of all kinds of goods. Here he worked as a lecturer and private tutor. He was the first person to give talks on **colour-blindness**, based on his own **affliction**. For many years, colour-blindness was called

atom 原子

brainchild
脑力劳动的产物

Quaker 贵格会教徒，是基督教新教的一个教派。

John Dalton
约翰·道尔顿英国化学家、物理学家、原子理论的提出者。

colour-blindness 色盲

affliction 苦难

"Daltonism". If you know someone who is colour-blind, it is probably a boy, since girls rarely suffer from it.

Dalton felt right at home at the Manchester Literary and Philosophical Society. Its active members became a kind of extended family for this shy man who never married. **Manchester's "Lit. & Phil."** was one of many similar societies established from the late eighteenth century in towns and cities throughout Europe and North America. **Benjamin Franklin**, the electrician, was one of the founders of the American Philosophical Society in Philadelphia. "Natural philosophy" was, of course, what we now call "science". The "Literary" in the Manchester society's name reminds us that science was not yet separated from other areas of intellectual activity; members would gather to hear talks on all sorts of subjects, from Shakespeare's plays to archaeology to chemistry. The age of specialisation, when chemists mostly talked to other chemists, or physicists just to other physicists, lay in the future. How exciting to range so broadly!

Dalton was a leading light in Manchester's scientific life, and his work was gradually appreciated throughout Europe and North America. He did some important experimental work in chemistry, but his reputation then and now rested on his idea of the chemical atom. Earlier chemists had shown that when chemicals **react with** each other, they do so in predictable ways. When **hydrogen** "burns" in ordinary air (part of which is **oxygen**) the product is always water, and if you measure things carefully, you can see that the **proportions** of the two gases that combine to form water are always the same. (Don't try this at home, because hydrogen is very easily burned, and can explode.) This same kind of regularity also happened in other chemical experiments with gases, liquids and solids. Why?

For **Lavoisier**, in the previous century, this was because elements were the basic units of matter and simply couldn't be broken down into smaller parts. Dalton called the smallest unit of matter the "atom". He insisted that the atoms of one element are all the same, but different from the atoms of other elements. He thought of atoms as extremely small, solid bits of matter, surrounded by heat. The heat around the atom served to help him explain how his atoms, and the

---

Lit. & Phil.
特指曼彻斯特文学与哲学学会

Benjamin Franklin
本杰明·富兰克林（1706—1790），美国政治家、物理学家和社会活动家，曾进行多项关于电的实验，发明避雷针，并最早提出电荷守恒定律，在研究大气电方面做出贡献。

react with 同……起反应
hydrogen 氢气
oxygen 氧气
proportion 比例

Antoine-Laurent de Lavoisier
安托万·洛朗·拉瓦锡（1743—1794），法国著名化学家、生物学家，被后世尊称为"现代化学之父"。

compounds they make when joined with other atoms, could exist in various states. For example, atoms of hydrogen and oxygen could exist as solid ice (when they had the least heat), or as liquid water, or as water **vapour** (when they had the most heat).

vapour 蒸汽

Dalton made models with little **cut-outs** to stand for his atoms. He marked his cardboard cut-outs with symbols, to save space (and time) when writing the names of **compounds** and their reactions (just as if he were sending a modern text message). At first his system was far too awkward to be used easily, but it was the right idea, so gradually chemists decided to use initials as the symbols for elements (and therefore Dalton's atoms). So, hydrogen became "H", oxygen "O", and carbon "C". Another letter sometimes had to be added to avoid confusion: for example, when helium was discovered later, it couldn't be H so became "He".

cut-out 缺口

compound 化合物

The beauty of Dalton's atomic theory was that it allowed chemists to know things about these bits of matter that they could never actually see. If all the atoms in an element are the same, then they must weigh the same, so chemists could measure how much one weighed compared to another. In a compound made of different kinds of atoms, they could measure how much of each atom there was in the compound, by relative weight. (Dalton couldn't actually measure how much an individual atom weighed, so atomic weights were merely compared with the weights of other atoms.) Dalton led the way here, and he didn't always get it right. For instance, when oxygen and hydrogen combine to form water, he assumed that one atom of hydrogen and one atom of oxygen were involved. Based on his careful weighing, he gave the atomic weight of hydrogen as 1 (hydrogen was the lightest known element), and the atomic weight of oxygen as 7, so he said they had a weight ratio of 1 to 7, or 1 : 7. He always **rounded** his atomic weights to whole numbers and the comparative weights he was working with suggested he was right. In fact, the weight ratios in water are more like 1 : 8. We also now know that there are two atoms of hydrogen in each **molecule** of water, so the ratio of atomic weights is actually 1 : 16—one for hydrogen to sixteen for oxygen. The current atomic weight of oxygen is 16. Hydrogen has retained the magical weight of 1, which Dalton gave

round 四舍五入

molecule 分子

it. Hydrogen is not only the lightest atom; it is also the most common one in the universe.

Dalton's atomic theory made sense of chemical reactions, by showing how elements or atoms combine in definite proportions. So, hydrogen and oxygen do this when they form water, and carbon and oxygen when they make **carbon dioxide**, and nitrogen and hydrogen when they make **ammonium**. Such regularity and consistency, as well as increasingly accurate tools for measurement, made chemistry a **cutting-edge** science in the early nineteenth century. Dalton's atomic theory provided its foundation.

Humphry Davy (1778—1829) was at the centre of this chemistry. Whereas Dalton was quiet, Davy was **flamboyant** and socially ambitious. Like Dalton, he came from a working-class background, and went to a good local school in Cornwall. He was lucky, too. He was apprenticed to a nearby doctor who was to train Davy to become a family doctor. Instead, Davy used the books that his master owned to educate himself in chemistry (and foreign languages). He moved to Bristol, becoming an assistant in a special medical institution that used different gases to treat patients. While there, Davy experimented with **nitrous oxide**—called "laughing gas" because when you breathed it, it made you want to laugh. Davy's book on the gas, published in 1800, caused a **sensation**, for nitrous oxide had become a "recreational drug" and nitrous oxide parties were all the rage. Davy also noted that, after breathing the gas, you didn't feel pain, and suggested that it might be useful in medicine. It took forty years before doctors took up his suggestion, and the gas is still sometimes used as an **anaesthetic** in modern dentistry and medicine.

Only the great city of London could satisfy Davy's ambitions. He got his chance to become lecturer in chemistry at the Royal Institution, an organisation that brought science to the middle-class public. Davy the showman thrived there. His talks on chemistry attracted large crowds—people often went to lectures for fun as well as to learn. Davy became a professor at the Institution, and his research flourished. Along with other chemists, he discovered the chemical use of **Volta's** electrical "pile", the first battery. He dissolved compounds in liquids to make solutions and then used

carbon dioxide 二氧化碳

ammonium 铵

cutting-edge 尖端的

Humphry Davy
汉弗里·戴维，英国化学家。

flamboyant 显眼的

nitrous oxide 一氧化二氮

sensation 轰动

anaesthetic 麻醉剂

Alessandro Volta
亚历山德罗·伏特（1745—1827），意大利物理学家，因在1800年发明伏打电堆而著名，后来他受封为伯爵。

the pile to pass an electric current through them, analysing what happened. What he saw is that in many solutions, the elements and compounds were attracted to either the negative or the positive ends (poles) of the pile. Davy identified several new elements this way: **sodium** and **potassium**, for instance, which both accumulated around the negative pole. Sodium is part of the compound **sodium chloride**, the substance that makes the ocean salty, and which we put on our food. Once new elements were discovered, Davy could experiment with them, and work out their relative atomic weights.

sodium 钠

potassium 钾

sodium chloride 食盐；氯化钠

Volta's pile, with its positive and negative poles, also changed the way chemists thought about atoms and chemical compounds. Positively charged things went towards the negative pole, and negatively charged ones to the positive pole. This helped explain why elements had natural tendencies to combine with each other. The Swedish chemist **Jöns Jacob Berzelius** (1779—1848) made this fact central to his famous theory of chemical combination. Berzelius survived a difficult childhood. Both his parents died when he was young and he was brought up by various relatives. But he grew up to become one of the most influential chemists in Europe. He discovered the joys of chemical research when he was training to be a doctor, and was able to work as a chemist in the Swedish capital, Stockholm, where he lived. He also travelled a lot, particularly to Paris and London—exciting places for a chemist.

Jöns Jacob Berzelius
永斯·雅各布·贝采利乌斯，瑞典化学家和伯爵，现代化学命名体系的建立者。

Like Davy, Berzelius used the Voltaic pile to look at compounds in solution. He discovered several new elements this way, and he published lists of them with ever more accurate atomic weights. He worked out the weights by carefully analysing the relative weights of substances combining to make new compounds, or by **breaking down** compounds and then carefully measuring the products. His chemical table of 1818 listed the atomic weights of forty-five elements, with hydrogen still as 1. It also gave the known compositions of over 2,000 compounds. It was Berzelius who popularised Dalton's convention of identifying elements by the first one or two letters of their name: C for carbon, Ca for **calcium**, and so on. This made the language of chemical reactions much easier to read. When compounds have more than one atom of an element in them, he indicated it with a number

break down 分解

calcium（化学元素）钙

following the letter. Berzelius placed the number above the letter, but scientists now put it below: O_2 means there are two atoms of oxygen. Apart from that, Berzelius wrote **chemical formulas** much as we do today.

chemical formulas [化学] 化学式

inorganic 无机的

organic 有机的

protein 蛋白质

Berzelius was much better with **inorganic** compounds than with **organic** ones. "Organic" compounds are ones containing carbon and are associated with living things: sugars and **proteins** are two examples. Organic compounds are often more complex chemically than inorganic ones, and they tend to react in rather different ways than the acids, salts and minerals that Berzelius was mostly examining. Berzelius thought that the reactions that go on in our bodies (or those of other living things such as trees and cows) could not be explained in quite the same way as those that happen in a laboratory. Organic chemistry was being developed during his lifetime in France and Germany, and although he distanced himself from these chemists, he actually contributed to their research. First, he provided the word "protein" to describe one of the most important kinds of organic compounds. Second, he realised that many chemical reactions will not take place unless there is a third substance present. He called this third thing a "**catalyst**". It helped the reaction—often by speeding it up—but it did not actually change during the reaction, unlike the other chemicals that combined or broke down. Catalysts are found throughout nature, and trying to understand how they work has been the goal of many chemists since Berzelius's time.

catalyst 催化剂

Elsewhere in Europe, "atoms" were helping chemists understand their work. There were still a lot of puzzles, however. In 1811, in Italy, the physicist **Amedeo Avogadro** (1776—1856) made a bold statement. It was so bold that it was neglected by chemists for almost forty years. He declared that the number of particles of any gas in a fixed volume and at the same temperature is always **identical**. "Avogadro's hypothesis", as it came to be called, had important consequences. It meant that the **molecular** weights of gases could be calculated directly, using a formula he devised. His idea, or hypothesis, also helped modify Dalton's atomic theory, because it explained a curious feature of one of the most studied gases, water vapour. Chemists had long puzzled why the volume of hydrogen and oxygen in a particular

Amedeo Avogadro 阿莫迪欧·阿伏伽德罗，意大利物理学家和化学家。

identical 完全相同的

molecular 分子的；与分子有关的

amount of water vapour was incorrect if one assumed one atom of hydrogen and one of oxygen combined to make a molecule of water. It turned out that there were two atoms of hydrogen for every atom of oxygen in water vapour. Chemists discovered that many gases, including both hydrogen and oxygen, exist in nature not as single atoms but as molecules: two or more atoms joined together: H_2 and O_2, as we would say.

Avogadro's ideas didn't seem to make sense, if you believed Dalton's atomic theory, and Berzelius's idea of the atoms of elements having definite negative or positive characteristics. How could two negative oxygen atoms bind together? These problems meant that Avogadro's work was neglected for a long time. Much later on, though, it made sense of many chemical puzzles and is now fundamental to our understanding of the chemist's atom. Science is often like that: all the pieces only fit together after a long time and then things start to make sense.

(2,260 words)

❶ Recall

Answer the following questions with the information from the passage.

1. What is another name for colour-blindness and how did it get this name?
2. Which atom is the lightest and the most common one in the universe? What is its atomic weight?
3. What is another name for nitrous oxide?
4. What is nitrous oxide used for in modern dentistry and medicine?
5. What are organic compounds?
6. Whose theory can explain the curious feature of water vapour?

❷ Interpret

Answer the following questions by analysing the passage.

7. At the end of Paragraph 4, the author asks the question, "This same kind of regularity also happened in other chemical experiments with gases, liquids and solids. Why?" What does *regularity* refer to? What were Lavoisier's and Dalton's answers to this question?

8. How did the modern atomic theory develop? Name the main chemists and their contributions.

Evaluate & Connect

Answer the following question by relating the passage to your own experience.

9. John Dalton said, "If I have succeeded better than many who surround me, it has been chiefly—may I say almost solely—from universal assiduity." On the basis of the well-known chemists introduced in Text A, please discuss what personality traits chemists have.

Text B

Background Information

This article is an excerpt from *The Disappearing Spoon: And Other True Tales of Madness, Love, and the History of the World from the Periodic Table of the Elements* published in 2010 by Little, Brown and Company. The book was authored by Sam Kean. Bill Streever (author of *Cold*) commented, "*The Disappearing Spoon* shines a welcome light on the beauty of the periodic table. Follow plain-speaking and humorous Sam Kean into the intricate geography and stray into astronomy, biology, and history, learn of neon rain and gas warfare, meet both ruthless and selfless scientists, and before it is over fall head over heels for the anything but arcane subject of chemistry."

Chemistry Way, Way Below Zero

Sam Kean

There's always something novel to discover about the elements, even today. But with most of the easy pickings already plucked by **Röntgen**'s time, making new discoveries required drastic measures. Scientists had to **interrogate** the elements under increasingly severe conditions—especially extreme cold, which **hypnotizes** them into strange behaviours. Extreme cold doesn't always **portend** well for the humans making the discoveries either. While the latter-day heirs of **Lewis and Clark** had explored much of Antarctica by 1911, no human being had ever reached the South Pole. Inevitably, this led to an epic race among explorers to get there first—which led just as inevitably to a grim cautionary tale about what can go wrong with chemistry at extreme temperatures.

That year was chilly even by **Antarctic** standards, but a band of pale Englishmen led by **Robert Falcon Scott** nonetheless determined that they would be the first to reach ninety degrees south latitude. They organized their dogs and supplies, and a **caravan** set off in November. Much of the caravan was a support team, which cleverly

---

Röntgen 伦琴（1845—1932），德国物理学家，X射线的发现者。

interrogate 审问，讯问

hypnotize 对……施催眠术

portend 预示，预兆

Lewis and Clark expedition 刘易斯与克拉克远征（1804—1806），美国国内首次横越大陆西抵太平洋沿岸的往返考察活动。

Antarctic 南极的

Robert Falcon Scott 罗伯特·福尔肯·斯科特（1868—1912），英国海军上校，被英国人称为20世纪初探险时代的伟大英雄。

caravan 旅行队

dropped caches of food and fuel on the way out so that the small final team that would dash to the pole could retrieve them on the way back.

Little by little, more of the caravan **peeled off**, and finally, after **slogging** along for months on foot, five men, led by Scott, arrived at the pole in January 1912—only to find a brown pup tent, a Norwegian flag, and an annoyingly friendly letter. Scott had lost out to Roald Amundsen, whose team had arrived a month earlier. Scott recorded the moment curtly in his diary: "The worst has happened. All the daydreams must go." And shortly afterward: "Great God! This is an awful place. Now for the run home and a desperate struggle. I wonder if we can do it."

Dejected as Scott's men were, their return trip would have been difficult anyway, but Antarctica threw up everything it could to punish and harass them. They were **marooned** for weeks in a monsoon of snow flurries, and their journals (discovered later) showed that they faced starvation, scurvy, dehydration, hypothermia, and gangrene. Most devastating was the lack of heating fuel. Scott had trekked through the Arctic the year before and had found that the leather seals on his **canisters** of **kerosene** leaked badly. He'd routinely lost half of his fuel. For the South Pole run, his team had experimented with **tin**-enriched and pure tin solders. But when his **bedraggled** men reached the canisters awaiting them on the return trip, they found many of them empty. In a double blow, the fuel had often leaked onto foodstuffs.

Without kerosene, the men couldn't cook food or melt ice to drink. One of them took ill and died; another went insane in the cold and wandered off. The last three, including Scott, pushed on. They officially died of exposure in late March 1912, eleven miles wide of the British base, unable to get through the last nights.

In his day, Scott had been as popular as **Neil Armstrong**—Britons received news of his plight with gnashing of teeth, and one church even installed stained-glass windows in his honour in 1915. As a result, people have always sought an excuse to absolve him of blame, and **the periodic table** provided a convenient **villain**. Tin, which Scott used as solder, has been a prized metal since biblical

peel off 离开

slog 步履艰难地行进

dejected 情绪低落的

marooned 受困的

canister 筒；罐

kerosene 煤油

tin 锡（一种化学元素，符号为 Sn）

bedraggled 湿透或沾满污秽的

Neil Armstrong 尼尔·阿姆斯特朗，美国宇航员，1969 年 7 月登陆月球，成为第一个登上月球的地球人。

the periodic table 元素周期表

villain 祸首，元凶

times because it's so easy to shape. Ironically, the better metallurgists got at refining tin and purifying it, the worse it became for everyday use. Whenever pure tin tools or tin coins or tin toys got cold, a whitish rust began to creep over them like **hoarfrost** on a window in winter. The white rust would break out into **pustules**, then weaken and **corrode** the tin, until it crumbled and **eroded away**.

Unlike iron rust, this was not a chemical reaction. As scientists now know, this happens because tin **atoms** can arrange themselves inside a solid in two different ways, and when they get cold, they shift from their strong "beta" form to the crumbly, powdery "alpha" form. To visualize the difference, imagine stacking atoms in a huge crate like oranges. The bottom of the crate is lined with a single layer of spheres touching only tangentially. To fill the second, third, and fourth layers, you might balance each atom right on top of one in the first layer. That's one form, or **crystal structure**. Or you might nestle the second layer of atoms into the spaces between the atoms in the first layer, then the third layer into the spaces between the atoms in the second layer, and so on. That makes a second crystal structure with a different density and different properties. These are just two of the many ways to pack atoms together.

What Scott's men (perhaps) found out the hard way is that an element's atoms can spontaneously shift from a weak crystal to a strong one, or vice versa. Usually, it takes extreme conditions to promote rearrangement, like the **subterranean** heat and pressure that turn carbon from **graphite** into diamonds. Tin becomes **protean** at **56°F**. Even a sweater evening in October can start the pustules rising and the hoarfrost creeping, and colder temperatures accelerate the process. Any abusive treatment or deformation (such as dents from canisters being tossed onto hard-packed ice) can **catalyse** the reaction, too, even in tin that is otherwise **immune**. Nor is this merely a **topical** defect, a surface scar. The condition is sometimes called tin **leprosy** because it burrows deep inside like a disease. The alpha-beta shift can even release enough energy to cause audible groaning—vividly called tin scream, although it sounds more like stereo static.

The alpha-beta shift of tin has been a convenient chemical **scapegoat** throughout history. Various European cities with harsh

---

hoarfrost 白霜

pustule 脓疱；任何似脓疱的隆起

corrode 侵蚀

erode away 腐蚀

atom 原子

crystal structure 晶体结构

subterranean 地下的

graphite 石墨

protean 多变的

56°F（华氏度）约13.3摄氏度，转换公式为（华氏度 –32）× 5/9

topical 局部的

catalyse 催化

immune 免疫的；不受影响的

leprosy 麻风病

scapegoat 替罪羊

winters (e.g., **St. Petersburg**) have legends about expensive tin pipes on new church organs exploding into ash the instant the organist blasted his first chord. (Some pious citizens were more apt to blame the Devil.) Of more world historical consequence, when **Napoleon** stupidly attacked Russia during the winter of 1812, the tin clasps on his men's jackets reportedly (many historians dispute this) cracked apart and left the Frenchmen's inner garments exposed every time the wind kicked up. As with the horrible circumstances faced by Scott's little band, the French army faced long odds in Russia anyway. But **element fifty**'s changeling ways perhaps made things tougher, and impartial chemistry proved an easier thing to blame than a hero's bad judgment.

There's no doubt Scott's men found empty canisters—that's in his diary—but whether the **disintegration** of the tin solder caused the leaks is disputed. Tin leprosy makes so much sense, yet canisters from other teams discovered decades later retained their solder seals. Scott did use purer tin—although it would have to have been extremely pure for leprosy to take hold. Yet no other good explanation besides **sabotage** exists, and there's no evidence of **foul play**. Regardless, Scott's little band **perished** on the ice, victims at least in part of the periodic table.

Quirky things happen when matter gets very cold and shifts from one state to another. Schoolchildren learn about just three interchangeable states of matter—solid, liquid, and gas. High school teachers often toss in a fourth state, **plasma**, a superheated condition in stars in which **electron**s detach from their **nucleic** moorings and go roaming. In college, students get exposed to **superconductors** and **superfluid helium**. In graduate school, professors sometimes challenge students with states such as quark-gluon plasma or **degenerate matter**. And along the way, a few wiseacres always ask why **Jell-O** doesn't count as its own special state. (The answer? Colloids like Jell-O are blends of two states. The water and **gelatine** mixture can either be thought of as a highly flexible solid or a very sluggish liquid.)

The point is that the universe can accommodate far more states of matter—different micro-arrangements of particles—than are dreamed of in our provincial categories of solid, liquid, and gas. And these new states aren't hybrids like Jell-O. In some cases, the very distinction between mass and energy breaks down. **Albert Einstein** uncovered one such state while fiddling around with a few quantum mechanics equations in 1924—then dismissed his calculations and disavowed his theoretical discovery as too bizarre to ever exist. It remained impossible, in fact, until someone made it in 1995.

In some ways, solids are the most basic state of matter. (To be **scrupulous**, the vast majority of every atom sits empty, but the ultra-quick hurry of electrons gives atoms, to our dull senses, the persistent illusion of solidity.) In solids, atoms line up in a repetitive, three-dimensional array, though even the most blasé solids can usually form more than one type of crystal. Scientists can now **coax** ice into forming fourteen distinctly shaped crystals by using high-pressure chambers. Some ices sink rather than float in water, and others form not six-sided snowflakes, but shapes like palm leaves or heads of cauliflower. One alien ice, Ice X, doesn't melt until it reaches 3,700°F. Even chemicals as impure and complicated as chocolate form **quasicrystals** that can shift shapes. Ever opened an old **Hershey's Kiss** and found it an unappetizing tan? We might call that chocolate leprosy, caused by the same alpha-beta shifts that doomed Scott in Antarctica.

Crystalline solids form most readily at low temperatures, and depending on how low the temperature gets, elements you thought you knew can become almost unrecognizable. Even the aloof **noble gases**, when forced into solid form, decide that huddling together with other elements isn't such a bad idea. Violating decades of **dogma**, Canadian-based chemist Neil Bartlett created the first noble gas **compound**, a solid orange crystal, with **xenon** in 1962. Admittedly, this took place at room temperature, but only with platinum hexafluoride, a chemical about as caustic as a superacid. Plus xenon, the largest stable inert gas, reacts far more easily than the others because its electrons are only loosely bound to its nucleus. To get smaller, closed-rank noble gases to react, chemists had to drastically screw down the temperature and basically anesthetize them. **Krypton** put up a good fight until about –240°F, at which point

Albert Einstein
阿尔伯特·爱因斯坦（1879—1955），20世纪著名的理论物理学家、思想家及哲学家，也是相对论的创立者，是现代物理学及20世纪最重要的科学家之一。

scrupulous 严谨的

coax 巧妙地做一件事

quasicrystal 准晶体

Hershey' Kiss
好时巧克力，北美地区最大的巧克力及巧克力类糖果制造商。

crystalline solids 结晶体

noble gases 惰性气体

dogma 教条
compound 化合物
xenon 氙

krypton 氪

super-reactive fluorine can latch onto it.

Getting krypton to react, though, was like mixing baking soda and vinegar compared with the struggle to graft something onto argon. After Bartlett's xenon solid in 1962 and the first krypton solid in 1963, it took thirty-seven frustrating years until Finnish scientists finally pieced together the right procedure for **argon** in 2000. It was an experiment of **Fabergé** delicacy, requiring solid argon; **hydrogen** gas; **fluorine** gas; a highly reactive starter compound, caesium iodide, to get the reaction going; and well-timed bursts of **ultraviolet** light, all set to bake at a frigid –445°F. When things got a little warmer, the argon compound collapsed.

Nevertheless, below that temperature argon fluor hydride was a durable crystal. The Finnish scientists announced the feat in a paper with a refreshingly accessible title for a scientific work, "A Stable Argon Compound." Simply announcing what they'd done was bragging enough. Scientists are confident that even in the coldest regions of space, tiny **helium** and **neon** have never bonded with another element. So for now, argon wears the title belt for the single hardest element humans have forced into a compound.

Given argon's reluctance to change its habits, forming an argon compound was a major feat. Still, scientists don't consider noble gas compounds, or even alpha–beta shifts in tin, truly different states of matter. Different states require appreciably different energies, in which atoms interact in appreciably different ways. That's why solids, where atoms are (mostly) fixed in place; liquids, where particles can flow around each other; and gases, where particles have the freedom to **carom** about, are distinct states of matter.

Still, solids, liquids, and gases have lots in common. For one, their particles are well-defined and discrete. But that **sovereignty** gives way to anarchy when you heat things up to the plasma state and atoms start to disintegrate, or when you cool things down enough and collectivist states of matter emerge, where the particles begin to overlap and combine in fascinating ways.

(2,041 words)

argon 氩

Fabergé 法贝热，以其精美卓绝的复活节珠宝彩蛋而闻名。第一颗皇室复活节彩蛋诞生于1885年的复活节。

hydrogen 氢

fluorine 氟

ultraviolet 紫外的；紫外线的

Helium 氦

Neon 氖

carom 碰撞

sovereignty 独立性；影响力

❶ Recall

Answer the following questions with the information from the passage.

1. Which element of the periodic table is believed to be responsible for Scott's failure?
2. Could you give an example of the alpha-beta shift of tin being used as a scapegoat (Paragraph 9)?
3. Why does Jell-O not count as a special state?
4. What is the most basic state of matter?
5. Why do scientists not consider noble gas compounds, or even alpha-beta shifts in tin, to be truly different states of matter?

❷ Interpret

Answer the following questions by analysing the passage.

6. In Paragraph 8, the author says, "What Scott's men (perhaps) found out the hard way is that an element's atoms can spontaneously shift from a weak crystal to a strong one, or vice versa." Read Paragraphs 6–8 to find out: How does tin (atoms) shift? And under what extreme conditions does tin become protean?
7. In Paragraph 14, the author says, "depending on how low the temperature gets, elements you thought you knew can become almost unrecognizable." What does this mean? Please explain it using the example of noble gases.

❸ Evaluate & Connect

Answer the following question by relating the passage to your own experience.

8. Chemistry is an incredibly fascinating field of study. Based on Text B and your own knowledge, please elaborate on why students today should study chemistry.

Unit 4

Science as Inquiry

Synopsis

  一些美国学者在 20 世纪 90 年代考察美国科学教育史时，不无感慨地说："如果非要用某个词语来描述近 30 年来美国科学教育工作者所努力追求的目标，这个词一定是'探究'。"自约翰·杜威 1909 年提出科学方法和思维的重要性到现在已有一个世纪之久，在这一百多年间人们对于科学探究的追求从未停止过，"以科学探究为核心"已成为国际基础科学教育的共识和各国科学教育改革的方向。那么"探究"这一概念指什么？如何实施"探究式教学"或"探究式学习"？这些是本单元探讨的重点问题。其中 Text A 描述 20 世纪"探究"概念的演变进程，激发读者思考探究的含义；Text B 通过对比一个地质学家与一个五年级班级的师生科学探究的经历，描述了探究的多重形式，有助于读者认识科学探究的过程。

Warm-up

Humans, especially children, are naturally curious. Many great scientific inventions and discoveries first started from scientists' curiosity about some unusual observations of nature, which led to their inquiry process. Below are some observations by famous scientists. Do you know what inventions or discoveries their observations led to? Are you familiar with their inquiry process? How did they arrive at their final discovery?

1. Archimedes noticed that water spilled over the edge of the bathtub as he got in and the more his body sunk into the water, the more water was displaced.

2. In a church, Galileo noticed that the lamp hanging above his head was swinging back and forth evenly.

3. Robert Boyle found that blue solutions (溶液) obtained from plants, such as syrup of violets (紫罗兰糖浆), are turned red by acids.

4. Lu Ban cut his hand on the blades of grass and then noticed the sharp teeth on the blades.

Text A

Background information

This article is extracted from the *Journal of Science Teacher Education*. It was written by Lloyd H. Barrow, an emeritus professor of the College of Education and Human Development at the University of Missouri, and published in 2006. This article describes how interpretations of inquiry have changed during the 20th Century. These multiple meanings have resulted in confusion among teachers of science and various interpretations by science teacher educators. The aim of this article is to help reach consensus about what inquiry is.

A Brief History of Inquiry: From Dewey to Standards

Lloyd H. Barrow

According to Webster's Third International Dictionary, inquiry is an "act or an instance of seeking for truth, information, or knowledge; investigation; research; or a question or query", while the root word *inquire* means "to ask for information about, to make an investigation or search, to seek information or questioning". Sometimes inquiry is spelled with an *I*, other times an *E*, reflecting a difference in the American and English spelling; either way, they mean the same thing—based upon question(s) asked by the learner or investigator. However, there is a lack of agreement on the meaning of inquiry in the field of science education. The purpose of this paper is to provide a historical timeline that illustrates how the concept of inquiry has evolved.

Early historical perspective

The inclusion of inquiry into **K-12** science curriculum was recommended by **John Dewey**, a former science teacher. Dewey considered that there was too much emphasis on facts without enough emphasis on science for thinking and an attitude of the mind. Dewey

K-12 指从幼儿园（Kinder-garten）到 12 年级的教育，美国义务教育和基础教育阶段。

John Dewey
约翰 · 杜威（1859—1952），美国著名哲学家、教育家和心理学家，实用主义的集大成者，民主主义教育思想的实践者，美国进步主义教育运动代表，被誉为 21 世纪影响东西方文化最大的人物。

encouraged K-12 teachers of science to use inquiry as a teaching strategy where the scientific method was **rigid** and consisted of the six steps: sensing **perplexing** situations, clarifying the problem, formulating a **tentative** hypothesis, testing the hypothesis, revising with **rigorous** tests, and acting on the solution. In Dewey's model, the student is actively involved, and the teacher has a role as facilitator and guide. In 1916, Dewey had encouraged that students be taught so that the students could be adding to their personal knowledge of science. To accomplish that, students must address problems that they want to know and apply it to the observable phenomena. Dewey's model was the basis for the Commission on Secondary School Curriculum (1937) entitled Science in Secondary Education. In 1944, Dewey modified his earlier interpretation of the scientific method to accomplish his goal of reflective thinking: presentation of the problem, formation of a hypothesis, collecting data during the experiment, and formulation of a conclusion. According to Dewey, problems to be studied must be related to students' experiences and within their intellectual capability; therefore, the students are to be active learners in their searching for answers.

Sputnik and inquiry

The launching of **Sputnik I** on October 4, 1957, caused the Nation to question the quality of the science teachers and the science curriculum used in schools. Earlier, the **National Science Foundation (NSF)** had funded the development of an innovative physics curriculum. The subsequent physics curriculum and other science curricula (biology, chemistry, physics, earth science, and elementary), with funding from NSF, provided for the development of curriculum and professional development for implementing the curriculum, with an emphasis on "thinking like a scientist". There was also an emphasis on science processes as individual skills (i.e., observing, classifying, inferring, controlling variables, etc.).

Joseph Schwab believed that students should view science as a series of conceptual structures that should be continually revised when new information or evidence is discovered. Earlier, Schwab (1960) had described two types of inquiry: stable (growing body of knowledge) and fluid (invention of new conceptual structures that

---

rigid 严格的；精准的
perplexing 使人困惑的
tentative 尝试性的
rigorous 严格的

Sputnik I
斯普特尼克 1 号，1957 年苏联发射的世界上第一颗人造卫星。

National Science Foundation (NSF)
美国国家科学基金会，成立于 1950 年，旨在通过资助基础科学研究计划，发展科学信息和增进国际科学合作等改进科学教育。

Joseph Schwab
约瑟夫·施瓦布（1909—1988），美国著名科学家、课程理论家和教育学家，倡导科学探究的教学和学习方式，推动了美国初等教育、中等教育和高等教育中以"科学探究"为核心的课程改革，也深刻影响了其他国家学校科学教育的变革和发展。

revolutionize science). He considered that science should be taught in a way that was to be consistent with the way modern science operates. He also encouraged science teachers to use the laboratory to assist students in their study of science concepts. He recommended that science be taught in an inquiry format. Besides using laboratory investigation to study science concepts, students could use and read reports or books about research and have discussions about problems, data, the role of technology, the interpretation of data, and any conclusions reached by scientists. Schwab called this "enquiry into enquiry".

Project Synthesis was a compilation of three major NSF sponsored projects—a review of 1955—1975 literature, case studies by Stake and Easley, and the 1977 national survey. In addition, other sources, such as Third Science National Assessment of Educational Progress results, were also used in developing a discrepancy model. There were four different goal clusters developed: personal needs, societal issues, academic preparation, and career education and awareness. The greatest emphasis (95%) was on academic preparation. Inquiry was one of the five areas of Project Synthesis. Inquiry was studied from two dimensions: a content for teachers and their students and the strategy used by science teachers to help their students learn science. The Project Synthesis report divided student outcomes for inquiry into three categories (science process skills, nature of scientific inquiry, and general inquiry process). Welch et al. recognized reasons that teachers do not use inquiry and identified limited teacher preparation, including management; lack of time, limited available materials; lack of support; emphasis only on content; and difficult to teach. Subsequently, Eltinge and Roberts (1993) identified three reasons for avoiding inquiry (state documents emphasizing content, easier to access content, and textbooks' emphasis of science as a body of knowledge).

Influence of policy documents

Project 2061, the long-term efforts by the American Association for the Advancement of Science (AAAS) to reform K-12 science, identified what all students should know and be able to do when they graduate at the end of 12th grade. Their first document, *Science*

Project Synthesis
项目综合，美国国家科学基金会资助的一项研究。其目的是解释和综合三项同样由 NSF 资助、关于科学教育状况的早期研究和科学国家教育进步评价产生的大量数据；通过检验科学教育期望状态和现实情况之间的差距，构建差异模型；基于检验结果对未来科学教育活动提出建议。该项目综合中共设立 5 个焦点组，分别从不同的角度解读数据，其中包括探究组（inquiry group）。

Project 2061
1985 年科学促进联合会（AAAS）发起有关数学、科学和技术的教育改革长期规划；在全国科学技术委员会的资助下，聘请了 400 位国内外科学家、教授、教师以及科学教育机构的负责人；1989 年，完成并公布了《2061 计划，面向全体美国人的科学》（SFAA）——一份关于数学、科学和技术知识目标的综合报告。

for All Americans* (SFAA), has a broad view in defining scientific literacy. Project 2061 established goals for the teaching of inquiry in the SFAA chapter entitled "Habits of the Mind", and inquiry was considered as a science content topic using the following recommendations: start with questions about nature, engage students actively, concentrate on the collection and use of evidence, provide historical perspective, insist on clear expression, use a team approach, do not separate knowledge from finding out, and deemphasize the memorization of technical vocabulary.

A second policy document, the ***National Science Education Standards*** [NSES, National Research Council (NRC), 1996] considers inquiry as the overarching goal of scientific literacy. It goes beyond Project 2061 in describing inquiry. First, inquiry is the first science content area that is viewed from two perspectives: what students should understand about scientific inquiry and the abilities students develop based on their experiences with scientific inquiry. Second, inquiry also includes the teaching strategies associated with inquiry-oriented science activities. Bybee (1997) argued that K-12 teachers of science should not separate science content from the processes of science. He encouraged the combining of science processes with scientific knowledge, reasoning, and critical thinking so students can develop a richer, deeper understanding of science.

Frequently, K-12 teachers of science have viewpoints about inquiry from the post-Sputnik era curriculum and original teacher preparation program, especially if they are **veteran** teachers of 10 or more years. Additional clarifications about what the NSES (NRC, 1996) meant when inquiry was discussed (content, process skills, or teaching strategies). According to the NRC (1996, 2000), K-12 teachers of science must know that inquiry involves (a) the cognitive abilities that their students must develop; (b) an understanding of methods used by scientists to search for answers for their research questions; and (c) a variety of teaching strategies that help students to learn about scientific inquiry, develop their abilities of inquiry, and understand science concepts. The following three paragraphs summarize interpretations about inquiry from the NRC in 1996, and each of these domains was clarified by the NRC in 2000.

NSES 美国科学教育史上第一个国家标准，与上文的 Project 2061 和全国科学教师协会的"中学科学的范围、程序和协调方案"（1992）并称为美国 90 年代三个国家级科学教育改革方案。

veteran 经验丰富的；老练的

The fundamental abilities of inquiry specified by the NRC (1996) are to:

1. identify questions and concepts that guide investigations (students formulate a testable hypothesis and an appropriate design to be used);

2. design and conduct scientific investigations (using major concepts, proper equipment, safety **precautions**, use of technologies, etc., where students must use evidence, apply logic, and construct an argument for their proposed explanations);

3. use appropriate technologies and mathematics to improve investigations and communications;

4. formulate and revise scientific explanations and models using logic and evidence (the students' inquiry should result in an explanation or a model);

5. recognize and analyse alternative explanations and models (reviewing current scientific understanding and evidence to determine which explanation of the model is best); and

6. communicate and defend a scientific argument (students should refine their skills by presenting written and oral presentations that involve responding appropriately to critical comments from peers).

Accomplishing these six abilities requires K-12 teachers of science to provide multi investigational opportunities for students. This type of investigation would not be a verification laboratory experience. When students practice inquiry, it helps them develop their critical thinking abilities and scientific reasoning, while developing a deeper understanding of science (NRC, 2000).

The second domain of inquiry is the understanding about inquiry so students will develop meaning about science and how scientists work. The six categories identified by the NRC (1996) are as follows:

1. conceptual principles and knowledge that guide scientific inquiries;

2. investigations undertaken for a wide variety of reasons—to discover new aspects, explain new phenomena, test conclusions of previous investigations, or test predictions of theories;

precaution 预防措施

3. use of technology to enhance the gathering and analysis of data to result in greater accuracy and precision of the data;

4. use of mathematics and its tools and models for improving the questions, gathering data, constructing explanations, and communicating results;

5. scientific explanations that follow accepted criteria of logically consistent explanation, follow rules of evidence, are open to question and modification, and are based upon historical and current science knowledge; and

6. different types of investigations and results involving public communication within the science community. (To defend their results, scientists use logical arguments that identify connections between phenomena, previous investigations, and historical scientific knowledge; these reports must include clearly described procedures so other scientists can replicate or lead to future research).

This domain of inquiry concentrates on how and why scientific knowledge changes when new evidence, methods, or explanations occur among members of the scientific community. Therefore, they will vary by grade level, but will be very similar, except with increasing complexity (NRC, 2000). Science methods courses need to provide future science teachers with exemplary examples of inquiry as a content area. The vast majority of their K-12 and college science laboratory experiences have not modelled inquiry as content. Teachers need to have inquiry modelled for them because they need to see the benefit for their future students.

The third domain of inquiry of the NSES is found in the teaching standards. There are several teaching strategies that **facilitate** students' developing a better understanding of science. Science teacher educators need to provide experiences and information so that future K-12 teachers of science can provide high-quality inquiry science lessons. Aspects of inquiry teaching include strategy to **assess** students' prior knowledge and ways to utilize this information in their teaching; effective questioning strategies, including open-ended questions; long-term investigations, rather than single-

facilitate 使便利；促进，推动

assess 评价，评估

period verification-type investigations, and so forth. To accomplish high-quality instruction, preservice students need to participate in **collaborative** learning opportunities. By pairing with similar observations in their field experiences with master teachers of science, they will develop a better personal model of how inquiry teaching facilitates students learning of science.

According to **Anderson** (2002), the last half of the 20th Century associated inquiry with "good science teaching and learning." His synthesis of the research about inquiry identified that both teachers and students must be considered. Anderson considered that science teacher's beliefs and values about students, teaching, and the purpose of education influence their adoption and **implementing** of inquiry. Specifically, he described three barriers or dilemmas that influence the implementation of inquiry.

1. Technical **dilemmas** include the ability to teach constructively; the degree of commitment to the textbook; the challenges presented by state assessments; the difficulties of implementing group work; the challenge of the new teacher role as a facilitator; the challenge of the new student role as an active, rather than a passive, learner; and inadequate professional development.

2. Political dilemmas (short-term or limited professional development programs, parental resistance that science is taught differently than they experienced, unresolved conflicts among science teachers about what and how to teach, lack of **available** resources, and differing views about failures) must be **addressed** at local and state levels because of funding **ramifications**.

3. Cultural dilemmas include quality of textbooks and support materials, views about purposes of assessment, and view of preparation for the next science class.

According to Anderson, these dimensions must be addressed systematically.

Using Anderson's (2002) dilemmas, there are a number of reasons that inquiry will not be enacted as recommended by such the policy documents as Project 2061 and the NSES (NRC, 1996). Some teachers could still have the belief that inquiry focuses upon

---

collaborative 合作的，协作的

Ronald Anderson 罗纳德·安德森，科罗拉多大学博尔德分校荣誉教授。专注于科学教育，主要研究领域为科学教育政策问题和科学教育改革。曾担任有重大影响力的科学教育研究协会（National Association for Research in Science Teaching）的主席。

implementing 实施，实行

dilemma 困境，难题

available 可用的

address 处理，设法解决

ramification 影响

single process skills. Therefore, they will need to understand the current view of the meaning of inquiry. This will require a significant amount of time for K-12 teachers, as well as higher education faculty to become competent in a standards-based approach for inquiry. According to **Caprio** (2001), the supervisor must also be comfortable with inquiry to be able to help their staff. According to **McIntosh** (2001), science faculty will need to modify their planning so that the science class has true course goals of content and inquiry. This will be labour intensive because it also requires students to modify their role (e.g., design their own experiments, report their findings to peers, etc.); and, because it will probably be different from their previous course work, teaching assistants will need to have extensive preparation.

Closing

Over the past century, science educators have provided multiple interpretations of inquiry. Consequently, K-12 teachers of science, students, and parents are confused. To help **clarify**, the NRC (2000) released Inquiry and the National Science Education Standards. This was done because many readers of the NSES were unclear about what inquiry means. Every inquiry must engage students in a scientifically oriented question. These questions must be of interest to the student; otherwise, they will not establish ownership. Science teachers who implement inquiry as described in this paper must be aware that students will require longer learning time because students bring to each investigation their current explanations and abilities (prior knowledge). However, research studies have shown that students will develop a deeper understanding of the science concepts when their prior knowledge is considered as they integrate new knowledge. Over the past century, inquiry had multiple meanings. I hope that, in the first decade of the 21st Century, we can reach consensus about what is inquiry by using the three domains of inquiry (abilities, understandings, and teaching strategies) as described by the NSES (NRC, 1996).

clarify 阐明，理清

(2, 358words)

❶ Recall

Answer the following questions with the information from the passage.

1. Why did John Dewey recommend the inclusion of inquiry into K-12 science curriculum?
2. What effects did the launching of *Sputnik I* have caused on science curricula?
3. In Project Synthesis, which two dimensions of inquiry were studied?
4. In what way does NSES go beyond Project 2061 in describing inquiry?
5. Which three dilemmas described by Anderson might influence the implementation of inquiry?

❷ Interpret

Answer the following questions by analysing the passage.

6. Which domain of inquiry in NSES has a similar meaning to what Schwab called "enquiry into enquiry"?
7. Compared with the earlier perspective of Dewey, how did the concept of inquiry evolve in NSES?

❸ Evaluate & Connect

Answer the following question by relating the passage to your own experience.

8. Do you have any suggestions for the implementation of inquiry in the classroom?

Text B

Background Information

This article is extracted from *Inquiry and the National Science Education Standards: A Guide for Teaching and Learning*, which was published by The National Academies Press in 2000. The guide book, written by the Committee on Development of an Addendum to the National Science Education Standards on Scientific Inquiry, builds on the discussion of inquiry in the National Science Education Standards to demonstrate how those responsible for science education can provide young people with the opportunities they need to develop their scientific understanding and ability to inquire. This article is the first chapter of the book, which describes the multiple roles of inquiry by comparing a geologist's scientific inquiry with that of a class of fifth-grade students and their enterprising teacher.

Inquiry in Science and in Classrooms

Students who use inquiry to learn science engage in many of the same activities and thinking processes as scientists who are seeking to expand human knowledge of the natural world. By describing inquiry in both science and in classrooms, this volume explores the many **facets** of inquiry in science education. Through examples and discussion, it shows how students and teachers can use inquiry to learn how to do science, learn about the nature of science, and learn science content. A good way to begin this investigation is to compare the methods and thinking process of a practicing scientist with the activities of an inquiry-based science lesson.

Inquiry in science

A geologist who was mapping **coastal deposits** in the state of Washington was surprised to discover a forest of dead **cedar** trees near the shore. A significant portion were still standing, but they clearly had been dead for many years. He found similar stands of dead trees at other places along the coast in both **Oregon** and **Washington**.

facet 方面

coastal deposits
沉积在海岸线附近、潮间带和水下岸坡上的所有松散的沉积物，如沙子、泥土等。

cedar 雪松

Oregon and Washington
俄勒冈州和华盛顿州，均位于美国西北部，太平洋沿岸。

He wondered, "What could have killed so many trees over so wide an area?"

Reflecting on his knowledge of earthquakes, **crustal plate boundaries**, and **subsidence** along coastlines, the geologist searched for possible explanations. "Did the trees die at the same time?" "Was their death related to nearby volcanic activity or some kind of biological **blight**?" "Given their coastal location, was there some relationship between the salt water and the destruction of the forests?"

He pursued his first question by dating the outer rings of the trees by using carbon 14 radiometric methods. He found that they all had died about 300 years ago. As for the cause of the trees' death, his mapping indicated no evidence for widespread volcanic deposits in the areas of dead forests. Furthermore, the trees were not burned, nor did careful examination indicate any evidence of insect infestation.

The geologist began thinking about the possible role of salt water in killing the trees. He recalled that a large section of the **Alaskan coast** dropped below sea level in 1964 when the **tectonic plate** that underlies much of the Pacific Ocean plunged beneath the North American tectonic plate that Alaska sits on as the result of a major "**subduction zone** earthquake". Many square miles of coastal forests in Alaska died when the coastline dropped and they were

---

crustal plate boundaries 地壳板块边界

subsidence （地面或建筑物的）下沉，沉降，下陷

blight（植物）枯萎病，疫病

Alaskan coast 阿拉斯加海岸

tectonic plate 构造板块

subduction zone 俯冲带。板块构造说认为，当大洋板块移动并与大陆板块相遇时，由于大洋板块岩石密度较大，地位也低，便俯冲到大陆板块之下，这一俯冲部分叫做俯冲带。

submerged in salt water following the earthquake. He knew that a similar subduction zone lies beneath the Washington and Oregon coast and **gives rise to** the volcanoes of the **Cascade mountains**. He wondered whether the trees in Washington and Oregon might have been drowned by sea water when a large section of the coast subsided during an earthquake 300 years ago.

To check this explanation, he collected more data. He examined the **sediments** in the area. Well-preserved sections of sediment exposed in the banks of streams inland from the stands of dead trees showed a clean layer of sand below the soil—unlike any of the dark, clay-rich soil above and below the sand. "Where did the white sand come from?" he wondered.

The geologist knew that subduction zone earthquakes often produce tsunamis—**tidal waves**. He thought the sand layer could be sand washed ashore during a tsunami. If so, this would be further evidence of a major coastal earthquake. Fossils recovered from the sand layer indicated the sand came from the ocean rather than being washed down from inland, supporting the tsunami hypothesis.

He published several articles in peer-reviewed scientific journals hypothesizing that the dead trees and sand layer found along the coast were evidence that a major earthquake occurred about 300 years ago, just before European settlers arrived in the region.

Several years later a Japanese **seismologist**, who was studying historic tide gauge records in Japan to document tsunamis from distant sources, identified a major earthquake somewhere along the Pacific **rim** on January 17, 1700, but the source of the earthquake was open to debate. Using historical records, he was able to eliminate the possibility of a large earthquake from most known earthquake source regions around the Pacific. Aware of the geologist's work on dead forests in the Pacific northwest, the Japanese seismologist suggested that the source of the tsunami was a large subduction zone earthquake beneath present day Oregon and Washington.

Now the geologist had more evidence supporting his explanation that the sand layer was caused by a tsunami that accompanied an earthquake. Further examination of coastal sediments uncovered

---

submerge 淹没

give rise to 引起；使发生

Cascade mountains 喀斯喀特山脉，北美洲环太平洋海岸山脉的一部分，位于美国西北部，由南向北从加州北部跨越俄勒冈州和华盛顿州。

sediment 沉淀物

tidal waves 海啸；浪潮

seismologist 地震学家

rim 边缘

additional, but older, remains of dead trees and sand layers. He now thinks that earthquakes producing very large tsunamis, like the one he first identified, have repeatedly struck the Pacific Northwest coast in the past thousand years, just as these large earthquakes strike other subduction zones beneath Japan, the Philippines, Alaska, and much of Western South America. The coastal subsidence caused by the earthquake submerged the trees in salt water, which led to their death.

As sometimes occurs with scientific research, the geologist's findings influenced public policy. Public officials have revised the building codes for Washington and Oregon, based on the deeper understanding of earthquakes that grew out of this research. New buildings must be designed to resist earthquake forces 50% larger than under the old code.

This story illustrates several important features of scientific inquiry. A scientist noticed a phenomenon and had the curiosity to ask questions about it. No doubt many other people had also noticed the dead trees, but they either did not wonder about the cause of death or were not in a position to answer the question. Using his knowledge of geology and what he learned about trees and their habitats, the geologist made connections between the dead trees and other features of the environment, such as the coastal location. Those questions guided his investigation, which included the use of carbon 14 methods to date the dead trees and the gathering of available knowledge about the geology of the region. He developed an explanation for the death of the trees based on this preliminary evidence and gathered more evidence to test his explanation. He then published articles in which he discussed the relationship between the evidence he accumulated and the explanation he proposed. Later, a scientist in another part of the world read the publications and, because scientists use universal descriptions and measurements, was able to compare his findings with those of the American scientist. The Japanese scientist obtained separate evidence—the occurrence of a tsunami on January 17, 1700—that gave further support to the hypothesis that a subduction zone earthquake occurring on that date led to the death of a large number of trees along the Pacific Northwest coast.

The nature of human inquiry

The geologist's search for understanding of the natural world is a good illustration of the human characteristics that make inquiry such a powerful way of learning. Humans are innately curious, as anyone knows who has watched a newborn. From birth, children employ **trial-and-error** techniques to learn about the world around them. As children and as adults, when faced with an unknown situation, we try to determine what is happening and predict what will happen next. We reflect on the world around us by observing, gathering, assembling, and synthesizing information. We develop and use tools to measure and observe as well as to analyse information and create models. We check and re-check what we think will happen and compare results to what we already know. We change our ideas based on what we learn.

trial-and-error 反复试验

This complex set of thinking abilities, which helped early humans gather food and escape danger, constitutes the highly developed capacity we refer to as inquiry. In recent human history, some people have directed their curiosity toward issues other than subsistence and survival—for example, the movement of **celestial objects**, the causes of seasons, the behaviour of moving objects, and the origins of organisms. Curiosity about such issues is unique to humans. People studied these phenomena, developing hypotheses and proposing explanations. The communication of hypotheses, ideas, and concepts among individuals shaped the strategies, rules, standards, and knowledge that we recognize today as scientific.

celestial objects 天体

Inquiry into the natural world takes a wide variety of forms. It can range from a child's wondering how it is possible for ants to live underground to the search by groups of physicists for new atomic particles. Inquiry in classrooms also takes a wide variety of forms, as described later in this volume. But whatever its exact form, its role in education is becoming an increasing focus of attention. Today the world is being profoundly influenced by scientific discoveries. People need to make and evaluate decisions that require careful questioning, seeking of evidence, and critical reasoning. Learning environments that concentrate on conveying to students what scientists already know do not promote inquiry. Rather, an emphasis on inquiry asks that we think about what we know, why we know, and how we have come to know.

Inquiry in the science classroom

One of the best ways to understand school science as inquiry is through a visit to a classroom where scientific inquiry is practiced. The following **vignette** features a particular grade, but classroom inquiry can and does happen at all grade levels.

vignette 小场景

Several of the children in Mrs. Graham's fifth grade class were excited when they returned to their room after recess one fall day. They pulled their teacher over to a window, pointed outside, and said, "We noticed something about the trees on the playground. What's wrong with them?" There were three trees growing side by side. One had lost all its leaves, the middle one had multi-coloured leaves—mostly yellow—and the third had lush, green leaves. The children said, "Why are those three trees different? They used to look the same, didn't they?" Mrs. Graham didn't know the answer.

Mrs. Graham knew that her class was scheduled to study plants later in the year, and this was an opportunity for them to investigate questions about plant growth that they had originated and thus were especially motivated to answer. Although she was uncertain about where her students' questions would lead, Mrs. Graham chose to take the risk of letting her students pursue investigations under her guidance. After all, they had had some experience last year in examining how seeds grow under different conditions. She hung up a large sheet of butcher paper where all the students could see it and said, "Let's make a list of ideas that might explain what's happening to those three trees outside." A forest of hands went up:

It has something to do with the sunlight.

It must be too much water.

It must not be enough water.

The trees look different. They used to look the same.

It's the season, some trees lose their leaves earlier than others.

There is poison in the ground.

The trees have different ages. One tree is older than the others.

Insects are eating the trees.

When the students were satisfied that they had enough ideas, Mrs. Graham encouraged them to think about which of their ideas were possible explanations that could be investigated and which were descriptions. She then invited each student to pick one explanation that he or she thought might be an answer. She grouped the students by choices: There was a "water group", a "seasons" group, an "insects" group, and so on. She asked each group to plan and conduct a simple investigation to see if they could find any evidence that answered their question. As they planned their investigations, Mrs. Graham visited each group of students and carefully listened as they formulated their plans. She then asked each group to explain their ideas to their classmates, resulting in further **refinement**. Using this quick and public assessment of where they were, she was able to help them think about the processes they were using to address their question and consider whether other approaches might work better.

refinement 改良，精炼

For the next three weeks, science periods were set aside for each group to carry out its investigation. Then groups used a variety of sources to gather information about characteristics of trees, their life cycles, and their environments. For example, the "different ages" group answered their question fairly quickly. They contacted the PTA members who were involved in planting that part of the playground and found the original receipts for the purchase of the trees. A check with the nursery indicated that all three trees were identical and of approximately the same age when purchased. As some groups completed their investigations early, Mrs. Graham invited their members to join other groups still in progress.

The water group decided to look at the ground around the trees every hour that they could. They took turns and jointly kept a journal of their individual observations. Since some students lived near the school, their observations continued after school hours and on weekends. They missed some hourly observations, but they had sufficient data to report to the class. "The tree without leaves is almost always standing in water, the middle tree is sometimes standing in water, and the green tree has damp ground but is never standing in water."

One of the students recalled that several months ago the leaves on one of his mother's **geraniums** had begun to turn yellow. She told him that the geranium was getting too much water. Mrs. Graham gave the group a pamphlet from a local nursery entitled "Growing Healthy Plants." The water group read the pamphlet and found that when plant roots are surrounded by water, they cannot take in air from the space around the roots and they essentially "drown." Based on their observations and the information they obtained from the pamphlet, the students concluded that the leafless tree was drowning, the middle tree was "kinda" drowning, and the third one was "just right."

The water group continued its work by investigating the source of the water. They found that the school **custodian** turned on a lawn sprinkler system three times a week. He left it running longer than necessary, and the excess water ran off the lawn and collected at the base of the trees. Since the ground was sloped, most of the water collected at one end of the tree-growing area. Together with the other groups, they reported their results to the rest of the class.

As different groups gave their reports, the class learned that some observations and information—such as those from the group investigating whether the trees were different—did not explain the observations. The results of other investigations, such as the idea that the trees could have a disease, partly supported the observations. But the explanation that seemed most reasonable to the students, that fit all the observations and conformed with what they had learned from other sources, was too much water. After their three weeks of work, the class was satisfied that together they had found a reasonable answer to their question. At Mrs. Graham's suggestion, they wrote a

geraniums 天竺葵

custodian 管理员

letter to the custodian telling him what they had found. The custodian came to class and thanked them. He said he would change his watering procedure and he did. Mrs. Graham then asked the students how they could find out if their explanation was correct. After some discussion they decided that they would have to wait until next year and see if all the trees got healthy again.

The following year, during the same month that they had observed the discrepancy, all three trees were fully clothed with green leaves. Mrs. Graham's former students were now even more convinced that what they had concluded was a valid explanation for their observations.

Parallels between inquiry in education and in science

One is struck by the parallels between Mrs. Graham's class and the inquiring geologist. The geologist began his investigation with a question about an unusual and intriguing observation of nature. So did Mrs. Graham's children. The scientist then undertook a closer examination of the environment—asked new and more focused questions—and proposed an explanation for what he observed, applying his knowledge of plate tectonics. The children applied their knowledge to **formulate** several explanations and new questions before undertaking further investigations. The scientist, knowing of investigations by other scientists, used their findings to confirm the validity of his original explanation. In Mrs. Graham's class, groups whose explanations were not confirmed lent strength to the "excess water" explanation. The geologist published his findings. The children "published" their findings in their reports to their classmates and later in a letter to the custodian. Although scientific research does not always influence public policy, the geologist's discoveries resulted in building code revisions in Washington and Oregon. The children's investigations led to revised lawn watering procedures at their school.

Inquiry in the classroom can take many forms. Investigations can be highly structured by the teacher so that students proceed toward known outcomes, such as discovering regularities in the movement of **pendulums**. Or investigations can be **free-ranging** explorations

formulate 制定

pendulums 钟摆
free-ranging 任意的

of unexplained phenomena, like the tree leaf discrepancies in Mrs. Graham's schoolyard. The form that inquiry takes depends largely on the educational goals for students, and because these goals are diverse, highly structured and more open-ended inquiries both have their place in science classrooms.

(2, 982 words)

❶ Recall

Answer the following questions with the information from the passage.

1. What surprising phenomenon did the geologist notice?
2. After careful thinking, what explanation did the geologist propose and how did he check it?
3. What new evidence provided by the Japanese seismologist supports the geologist's explanation?
4. What information did the water group obtain from the pamphlet?
5. What were the results of the children's investigations?

❷ Interpret

Answer the following questions by analysing the passage.

6. How did the geologist use inquiry to investigate the cause of the trees' death? Describe his scientific inquiry process by naming the important steps.
7. How did Mrs. Graham's class use inquiry to explore the reason why the three trees were different? Describe their scientific inquiry process by naming the important steps.
8. Can you find the parallels between Mrs. Graham's class and the inquiring geologist? Are there any other inquiry forms in the classroom?

❸ Evaluate & Connect

Answer the following question by relating the passage to your own experience.

9. Are you curious about any natural phenomena in your life? Recall how the geologist and Mrs. Graham's class used inquiry to explore the natural world and make a record of your own inquiry process.

My inquiry diary	
Step 1: I noticed a phenomenon.	...
Step 2: I reflected on my background/current knowledge about it.	...
...	...
...	...

Unit 5

Science as Human Endeavor

Synopsis

  如何才能成为一名优秀的科学家？社会影响在科学进步中扮演着什么样的角色？本单元对这些问题展开了深入探讨，促使读者思考科学研究与人类行为之间的复杂关系。Text A 介绍了一位为人谦逊、不善交际的科学家，南卡罗来纳大学生物学家奥斯汀·休斯，其执着、勤奋而严谨的治学求真精神深深地影响着他人；Text B 阐明了社会影响对于科学研究的重要性，纠正了社会因素阻碍科学进步的传统认知偏见。

Warm-up

The Chinese agriculturalist Yuan Longping was dubbed the "Father of Hybrid Rice" and awarded the Medal of the Republic. Professor Yuan was a pioneer in hybrid rice research and made remarkable achievements in this area, becoming the first to develop hybrid rice varieties in the 1970s. The achievements of Yuan Longping helped boost global food security, and provided food sources in areas with a high risk of famine. He was awarded the 2004 World Food Prize and 2004 Wolf Prize in Agriculture for his achievements as part of the Green Revolution in Agriculture.

Discuss Professor Yuan's contributions to the world and outstanding qualities as a great scientist with your partner. Then share what you can learn about scientific research from his story.

Text A

Background information

This text is excerpted from the article "The Humble Scientist" published in *The New Atlantis*. The author Chase W. Nelson was a biology doctoral student at the University of South Carolina when he published the article in 2015 to commemorate his mentor Austin L. Hughes (1949—2015). Professor Austin L. Hughes was a major contributor to evolutionary theory and practice, who contributed to two areas of molecular evolution: the role of positive (Darwinian) selection, and the impact of gene duplications during genome evolution. At the same time, Austin L. Hughes also revolutionized the study of selection at the nucleotide level, especially for immune system genes.

The Humble Scientist

Chase W. Nelson

A dear **atheist** friend once turned to me in the middle of a concert to whisper, "That's what holiness looks like." Shocked by her response to this musician, I later asked what she meant. "I think holiness is when someone finds what they most love to do in this life."

atheist 无神论者

The same can be said about the scientific work of University of South Carolina biologist **Austin L. Hughes**, my teacher, who died in October 2015 at the age of sixty-six. I have never met an intellectual more dedicated to an objective analysis of truth, despite what some might think of as conflicting commitments. A relatively conservative man, he spent his career studying evolution and contributing to its understanding with a single-minded tenacity and seriousness. He was first a philosophy student at Georgetown and Harvard in the late Sixties and early Seventies, but during his graduate years came to notice how preoccupied philosophy was with science while **eschewing** other kinds of knowledge, due especially to the influence

Austin L. Hughes 奥斯汀·休斯（1949—2015），在分子进化论领域做出了重要贡献，开创了自然选择对于基因编码的影响研究。

eschew 避开

of logical **positivism**. This drew his attention to the sciences, of which biology, it seemed to him, was an area of work relatively tolerant toward people of faith as compared to philosophy.

It turned out, as he explained in a 2013 interview with *Salvo* magazine, that the reason scientists seemed more tolerant at first "was just that they assumed that no one in their field **subscribed to** religion." Nevertheless, although it may now stretch **credulity** to imagine the word "humble" as an accurate descriptor of biology's attitude toward other disciplines, this was to him an important part of what drew him to study zoology, first at the University of Maryland, then at West Virginia University, and then at Indiana University, where he received his Ph.D. in 1984. In the pages of this journal, he recalled:

> When I decided on a scientific career, one of the things that appealed to me about science was the modesty of its practitioners. The typical scientist seemed to be a person who knew one small corner of the natural world and knew it very well, better than most other human beings living and better even than most who had ever lived. But outside of their **circumscribed** areas of expertise, scientists would hesitate to express an authoritative opinion. This attitude was attractive precisely because it stood in sharp contrast to the **arrogance** of the philosophers of the positivist tradition, who claimed for science and its practitioners a broad authority with which many practicing scientists themselves were uncomfortable.

His work in biology began with examinations of the behaviours of certain beetles, birds, and fishes, and also of human **kin** groups. He then broke into **molecular** evolution as a postdoctoral researcher under **Masatoshi Nei** at the University of Texas at Houston, where he met other molecular-evolutionary greats such as **Wen-Hsiung Li**. It was there too that he made one of his most influential contributions to science, in a paper coauthored with Nei in 1988, **demonstrating** a way to detect a form of positive Darwinian natural selection.

His writing was an act of worship of truth. One paper after another **poured forth**—some three hundred in total, plus two

---

positivism 实证论

subscribe to 信仰
credulity 轻信

circumscribe 限定
arrogance 傲慢
kin 亲戚；有血缘关系的
molecular 分子的
Masatoshi Nei
　　〔日〕根井正利（1931— ），国际著名分子进化学家与遗传学家，美国国家科学院院士。
Wen-Hsiung Li
　　李文雄（1942— ），著名分子进化生物学家，美国艺术与科学院院士和美国国家科学院院士。
demonstrate 证明
pour forth 涌出

books—addressing gene duplication, natural selection, and **phylogenetic** relationships as he investigated the evolutionary history of a wide swath of living things. His passion for this work earned him membership with the American Association for the Advancement of Science in 2010.

An extremely private person—we never once had dinner—Hughes's priorities were clearly faith, family, and science. He had little time to **bother with** anything else, even such trivialities as pleasant greetings. When happening upon him on or off campus, at most a quick nod or grunt might issue forth as he continued on his way. We who circled around him, **propelled** in our orbits by the mental inspiration he gave, learned not to **confuse** his brevity for anger or even disinterest. He was shy, and simply had more important things to do: a paper, a class, a coffee with his wife. It was clear that his heart went deeper than a casual acquaintance might notice. Speaking of personal failings, perhaps with family or friends, he once mused in a conversation that "things might have turned out differently if I'd written a hundred less papers—ah well, it's too late to change that now." If his devotion to family and church were any indication, the importance of love was a lesson he had learned well, as was the importance of tolerance. Despite the fact that I am a relatively outspoken gay activist and **Bernie Sanders** supporter, both undoubtedly in strong conflict with his views, these things never once altered his respect for or treatment of me. We simply found shared holy ground in our mutual passion for good science, and happily toiled together, whatever differences we might have had.

Despite his awkwardness in social settings, in lab meetings he could be talkative and energetic, if not downright **chipper**. No topic was exempt. After bringing everyone up to speed on research and setting a direction for the coming week, we would often speak about politics and philosophy. With his training in both philosophy and science, and his rich library of books in multiple languages, Professor Hughes had an **inexhaustibly** vast knowledge. If one topic failed to stimulate, he would find another. Once, while sitting behind him in a departmental biology lecture, I noticed him grow bored and **retrieve** a French philosopher from his bag, and he proceeded to read, in

French, the majority of a chapter before the talk finished. When we lost him, we lost a mentor not only in science but in many other subjects as well, and one with the rare ability to look beyond his own area of accomplishment to gain a fuller image of the world. Despite the independence his personality demanded of others, a certain repose could always be taken in the fact that, should all else fail, one could simply "ask Austin." His absence means, for me, a loss of that intellectual security. I may never find it again.

In his writing for more popular outlets, Hughes advanced a clear vision for the roles of science and faith in the human experience, as in his 2012 *New Atlantis* essay "The Folly of **Scientism**." Here he showed that science, far from being sufficient to address the broad range of questions once tasked to philosophy, is rather itself derivative of and dependent on philosophy. Defining "scientism" loosely as the view that science is the only sure means of acquiring knowledge of any sort, he writes:

scientism 科学主义，以自然科学技术为哲学基础，并视自然科学为哲学标准。

> In contrast to reason, a defining characteristic of superstition is the **stubborn** insistence that something—a **fetish**, an **amulet**, a pack of **Tarot cards**—has powers which no evidence supports. From this perspective, scientism appears to have as much in common with superstition as it does with properly conducted scientific research. Scientism claims that science has already resolved questions that are **inherently** beyond its ability to answer.

stubborn 顽固的

fetish 神物；偶像

amulet 护身符

Tarot cards 塔罗牌（预卜命运的一种牌）

inherently 内在地

His essay helped **spark** heated debates about scientism, including responses from some of its most **ardent** champions, such as Jerry Coyne and Steven Pinker, each of whom Hughes critiqued again thereafter. However, **contentious** claims about science seemed to bother him only when tied to some metaphysical agenda, such as Coyne's atheism. Conflict on other matters, for instance hostile rejections of his work overturning well-accepted bird **phylogenies**, prompted easy **resignation**: "Oh well, I tried."

spark 引发

ardent 热情的

contentious 引起争论的

phylogeny 系统发生学

resignation 放弃

Hughes was at his best—and sometimes quite controversial in field—when pushing back against certain claims about adaptive evolution. In a 2007 article in *Heredity*, **provocatively** titled "Looking

provocatively 引发争议地；煽动地

for Darwin all the wrong places: the misguided quest for positive selection at **nucleotide** sequence level," he called into question the "widespread use inappropriate statistical methods" that, he claimed, had produced a false impression about how molecular evolution works. Positive Darwinian natural selection—the favouring of advantageous mutations—is far common than is widely believed, he wrote, and "is unlikely to be involved in the evolution of major **morphological** and developmental adaptations." The controversial article led to the misperception among some in the field that Hughes had rejected the methods he had pioneered in the 1980s with Masatoshi Nei for detecting this form of selection. Rather, what he did was clarify the appropriate scope of their use in a time when other scientists sometimes seemed eager to grant an almost magical power to the role of selection in evolution.

The 2007 paper relied heavily on the work of **Motoo Kimura**, leading architect of the neutral theory of molecular evolution, which states that at the molecular level most genetic variations that **permeate** populations are "neutral" in the sense that they do not affect the organism's survival and reproduction. In the original draft of a magnificent 2009 paper about Kimura's theory, Hughes went so far as to say that Kimura was a figure more important than Darwin. As Hughes told me in one of our weekly meetings, one reviewer fiercely objected ("Whoa!"). The final publication is worded somewhat less strongly: "it is not an exaggeration to say that Kimura was the most important evolutionary biologist since Darwin." A 2011 review Hughes wrote in *Heredity* continued in this vein, proposing a mechanism that explains a great deal of adaptive evolution **without recourse to** natural selection at all. (In a letter to the editor, two researchers challenged the claims in this paper, but it does not appear that Hughes ever responded.) Why question positive natural selection? In a **podcast** discussion with *Heredity*, Hughes answers simply that "there really isn't all that much evidence that it actually happens to the extent to which it would be needed to explain all of the adaptive traits of organisms." Simple enough.

Hughes's greatest professional fault was **arguably** his lack of patience with slower thinkers. Over his roughly forty years working

---

nucleotide 核苷酸

morphological 形态学的

Motoo Kimura 木村资生（1924—1994），日本群体遗传学家和进化生物学家。

permeate 散布

without recourse to 不依靠

podcast 播客

arguably 可辩论地；可辩驳地

in biology, he took on only a handful of grad students, graduating only five Ph.Ds. Surely his **impersonal** tendencies had something to do with this. Neither was he **exempt** from frustration with himself. Once, trying to work out a question I had asked about population genetics, he put down the pen with some force and, visibly **exasperated**, exclaimed, "I'm just too stupid." Dissatisfaction with his own lack of understanding may be what drove his growth and **prowess** as an intellectual and scientist.	impersonal 客观的 exempt 获豁免的 exasperated 恼怒的 prowess 造诣
It will be difficult to carry on without his surprising outbursts ("Biologists are **morons**!" with a fist slamming the table), or especially without the stern look on his face that would quickly **dissolve into** a chuckle as he realized his own excess of passion. Hoping to write papers like his, I moved from New York to South Carolina in 2011 and will be ever changed as a result—for good. Would that we could all strive to pursue our goals with **a fraction of** his diligence, and to form our opinions with **an ounce of** his objectivity. His guidance will be sorely missed, but will live on in his writings and in those whose lives he touched.	moron 傻瓜 dissolve into 化作；转为 a fraction of 一点儿 an ounce of 一点儿
(1, 850 words)	

Recall

Answer the following questions with the information from the passage.

1. What does Nelson's atheist friend think of holiness?
2. According to Hughes, what's the different attitude between a typical scientist and a philosopher of the positivist tradition?
3. What did Hughes's papers address when he investigated the evolutionary history of a wide swath of living things?
4. What were Hughes's priorities?
5. What was Hughes like in social settings and lab meetings?
6. In Hughes's view, what's the relationship between science and philosophy?

Unit 5 Science as Human Endeavor

II Interpret

Answer the following questions by analysing the passage.

7. At the very beginning of Paragraph 10, the author says, "Hughes was at his best—and sometimes quite controversial in field—when pushing back against certain claims about adaptive evolution." Why was Hughes controversial in the field of adaptive evolution?

8. In Paragraph 11, the author states, "In the original draft of a magnificent 2009 paper about Kimura's theory, Hughes went so far as to say that Kimura was a figure more important than Darwin." Please elaborate the reasons why Hughes thought so highly of Kimura.

III Evaluate & Connect

Answer the following question by relating the passage to your own experience.

9. "Dissatisfaction with his own lack of understanding may be what drove his growth and prowess as an intellectual and scientist." Ponder how dissatisfaction with your own lack of understanding is relevant to your growth and success.

Text B

Background Information

This text was co-authored by Maarten Boudry and Massimo Pigliucci. Maarten Boudry teaches philosophy at Ghent University, Belgium, and he has published articles in such journals as *Philosophy of Science*, *Philosophia*, *Quarterly Review of Biology*, *Science & Education*, and *Philosophical Psychology*. Massimo Pigliucci is the K. D. Irani Professor of Philosophy at the City College of New York, whose research interests cover the philosophy of science, evolutionary biology, the history and structure of evolutionary theory, and the relationship between science and philosophy. Their co-edited books include *Philosophy of Pseudoscience: Reconsidering the Demarcation Problem* (2013) and *Science Unlimited? The Challenges of Scientism* (2017). The present article is adapted from Chapter 13 in *Perspectives on Science and Culture* edited by Kris Rutten, Stefaan Blancke, and Ronald Soetaert, which was published on Feb. 15, 2018 by Purdue University Press.

Vindicating Science—By Bringing It Down

Maarten Boudry and Massimo Pigliucci

What is the role of the social in science? If one consults science textbooks, one will find that the social dimension of scientific knowledge is **conspicuously** absent. Science is supposed to reflect the way the world really is, independent of our petty human lives. It is, in the classical view, the **epitome** of a rational endeavour, free from social influences. Of course, science is carried out by human beings, but their individual backgrounds and social lives are simply taken to be irrelevant. Individual scientists are effaced from the fruits of their intellectual labours, or **relegated** to historical footnotes. What matters are the intellectual merits of a theory, not who conceived it. What matters is the evidence, not who gathered it.

In recent decades, sociologists and historians have tried to bring science back to earth, but many of them have **unwittingly** bought

conspicuously	明显地
epitome	缩影
relegate	使降级
unwittingly	不经意地

into the same simplistic opposition. Social influences on science have been **relished** by its cynical critics and resisted by its admirers, and for the same reason: the fear (or hope) that it would destroy the credentials of science. In what follows, we discuss the historical roots of this opposition. We also point to a deeper cognitive explanation for this battle over the social nature of science: our basic intuition that rationally justified beliefs are not in need of any explanation, and that only false and foolish ones are.

Explaining rational belief

Not all beliefs held by our fellow human beings appear to produce an epistemic **itch**. People believe that dolphins are mammals, and that the earth orbits the sun, but we rarely wonder how they arrived at such **homely** truths. Beliefs such as these are just obvious, and no sane person would dispute them. Not only are we not interested in how other people came to hold these beliefs, we are also **oblivious** to how we did so ourselves. Where did you acquire the belief that dolphins are mammals, or that the earth goes around the sun? Your sources for these convictions, though you surely must have had them, are hard to track down.

Psychologists distinguish between **episodic memories** and **semantic memories**. Episodic memories carry a mental source tag, containing the time, place, and situation where we acquired them. Semantic memories, by contrast, are floating unanchored in our mental space: we can no longer retrieve the moment in our lives when we first learned that dolphins are mammals, although surely there must have been such a moment. Knowledge about biological **taxonomy** is not innate, and in fact, as in the case of dolphins, it is often surprising and counterintuitive.

There are good reasons why our brains don't bother to keep a source tag for semantic memories: doing so would just clog our memory, and be a waste of brain resources. Take the belief that coal is black. People may have acquired this knowledge in any number of ways: some may have learned about **soil deposits** and compression of organic matter in elementary school, others had first-hand experience with the substance as a child, before learning about its origins. Still

---

relish 喜欢

itch 痒；渴望

homely 平凡的

oblivious 没意识到的

episodic memory 情景记忆

semantic memory 语义记忆

taxonomy 分类法

soil deposits 土壤沉积

others may have learned about coal from the accounts of parents or friends. None of this is consequential for the end result: the culturally shared knowledge of a black, solid, combustible material called "coal".

Down to earth

In the idealized conception of science, which focuses on the successful end result of scientific activity, there is no place for any influence of the social, or indeed, for any of the actors involved in the scientific endeavour. All of that is swept under the carpet. But the fact that the eventual goal of science is to eliminate the social does not imply that social factors have no important role to play in the process. Science, after all, is nothing but the **concerted** effort of (sometimes not so) humble human brains, none of which was designed to **unravel** the mysteries of the world on its own.

In *The Structure of Scientific Revolutions*, Thomas Kuhn famously argued that the history of science can be divided into periods of normal science, **punctuated** by episodes of revolution. During times of **normal science**, all scientists work within a certain paradigm, sharing background knowledge, methodologies, experimental procedures, and rules of inference. Nobody questions the validity of the reigning paradigm. The period of normal science ends when a critical level of "anomalies" has accumulated, that is, empirical and conceptual problems that the ruling paradigm has trouble dealing with. This crisis eventually leads to a revolution and a paradigm shift, after which normal science resumes again.

In periods of normal science, uncritical acceptance of the reigning paradigm is ensured through social conformity and transferred from the old generation to the new. During the revolutionary period, in Kuhn's picture, the social dynamics of science are even more important. This is because the old and the new paradigm, according to Kuhn, are "**incommensurable**," meaning that the choice of one paradigm over the other cannot be settled by rational means. It is akin to a **gestalt** switch, where two different conceptual frameworks offer a completely different perspective on a given phenomenon.

---

concerted 协调一致的

unravel 解开；阐明

punctuate 间隔

normal science 常态科学

incommensurable 不能相比的

gestalt [德] 格式塔，（心理）形态（经验之统一的全体）

Many philosophers of science **dismissed** Kuhn's notion of paradigm shifts and incommensurability as a form of "mob psychology." In describing this gestalt switch between the old and the new, however, Kuhn opened up a space for social influences on science, which some sociologists have enthusiastically exploited and, to Kuhn's own dismay, pushed beyond what he himself thought reasonable. In the end, "whether a revolution occurs or the anomalies are simply ignored," as Golinski summarized, the approach of the radical sociologists "would depend on the social **configuration** of the community". Sociologists such as Harry Collins came to the rather surprising conclusion that "the natural world has a small or non-existent role in the construction of scientific knowledge".

There is a continuing debate about the legacy of Kuhn's work, and the correct interpretation of such ambiguous terms as "incommensurability" and "paradigm". In any case, as sociologists were following up on Kuhn's lead, philosophers of science tried to **reinstate** the distinction between the rational and the social, carving out a restricted **niche** for social explanations. The proper place for the social was mainly defined in a negative fashion. **Imre Lakatos**, who was attempting to incorporate Kuhn's insights into the **falsificationist** philosophy of his mentor **Karl Popper**, used the notion of "research program" as a unit of analysis of the history of science, a less **encompassing** concept than Kuhn's "paradigms". According to Lakatos, good science proceeds in a rational way, unless or until a scientific research program starts to **degenerate**. When science shows signs of such degeneration, we can no longer explain what happens in a purely rational fashion, and we must look for additional social and psychological accounts. In other words: when rationality breaks down, the sociologists are allowed to jump in the **fray**.

The truth of the matter is that all beliefs, the true and the false ones alike, have a causal history, involving cognitive and social factors (in varying combinations). If we want to understand how scientists have been able to **unearth** all sorts of true beliefs about the world, we need to understand what kinds of people scientists are, what kind of cognitive strategies they bring to bear on their research

---

dismiss 搁置；摒除，放弃

configuration 结构

reinstate 使恢复

niche 壁龛

Imre Lakatos
伊姆雷·拉卡托斯（1922—1974），匈牙利哲学家，以反形式主义的数学哲学和科学研究项目方法论而著名。

Karl Popper
卡尔·波普尔（1902—1994），20世纪最著名的哲学家之一，批判理性主义的创始人。他认为，经验观察必须基于理论指导，但理论本身又是可证伪的，因此其理论又被称为证伪主义。

falsificationist 证伪主义者

encompassing 包容的

degenerate 退化

fray 争论

unearth 发掘

questions, what the social organization of science is, and how hypotheses are tested and evaluated within a scientific community.

Naturalizing science

The simple opposition between the rational and the social-psychological explanations **goes against the grain** of naturalism. Scientific knowledge does not drop out of thin air: it is embodied in real human beings. If our best scientific theories in some way reflect the world out there, this must have come about through the usual perceptual capacities and cognitive operations, with available technological equipment, and in a complex network of social interactions. How else could it have come about?

| go against the grain 背道而驰 |

Science itself, after all, tells us that the human brain is a product of evolution by natural selection, and science the product of cultural evolution. Humans did not evolve to unravel the structure of the cosmos. Indeed, evolution has equipped us with a host of biases and intuitions that served our ancestors well in the environment in which they had to survive and reproduce, but that often get in the way of our modern quest to uncover the nature of the universe. The sociologists are right that science is a deeply social endeavour, and that all scientific knowledge is in this sense "socially constructed". No single individual **marooned** on a desert island, no matter how brilliant, would be capable of finding out any of the significant truths about the universe that we currently possess. Though the history of science has known some solitary geniuses, working in relative isolation from their peers, even they were still engaged in a collective enterprise, in the sense that they were building on the work of numerous predecessors. Isaac Newton was standing on the shoulders of giants.

marooned 陷于孤立无援困境的

The realization that science is a deeply social enterprise, and that scientific consensus is reached through **coalition** forming and competition, should not surprise us. The question is what particular social organization is exemplified by science, and whether this is **conducive** to its epistemic aspirations. Scientists are human beings, **warts and all**. If scientists collectively succeed in finding out significant truths about the universe, while other endeavour's have failed in this regard, this must have come about through the particular social dynamics of science.

coalition 联盟；联合

conducive 有益的
warts and all 毫无保留

Positive roles for the social

Many scientists believe that being objective and impartial are the **cardinal** virtues of science, and that bias and prejudice make one unsuitable for scientific work. Although the culture of science rightly encourages these virtues, they are by no means necessary for the success of science. Indeed, a certain **modicum** of bias in this or that direction may actually facilitate the progress of science.

It is not a problem that an individual scientist is biased, or emotionally attached to a particular hypothesis. The social organization of science makes sure that these biases will be balanced by others **tilting** in different directions. **Helen Longino**, for example, has put forth an account of the importance of epistemic diversity in the workings of science, arguing that (near) objectivity in scientific endeavours emerges from two sources: on the one hand, science constantly confronts itself with the reality of the world, as assessed by our best empirical methods. This leaves comparatively little room for alternative views. On the other hand, the more cultural, gender, and ideological diversity there is within the scientific community itself, the more likely it is that culture-, gender-, or ideology-specific biases will be corrected.

In general terms, a good social arrangement for finding out the truth of some matter is to have two or more competing groups pursue different hypotheses, trying their utmost to **garner** evidence for their own view and to prove competitors wrong. As **David Hull** writes, with regard to the ideal of objectivity in science: "The objectivity that matters so much in science is not primarily a characteristic of individual scientists but of scientific communities. Scientists rarely refute their own pet hypotheses, especially after they have appeared in print, but that is all right. Their fellow scientists will be happy to expose these hypotheses to severe testing". In other words, it is best to let a thousand flowers bloom in science. Even if you think some hypothesis is unlikely and **far-fetched**, it might still be worthwhile for some scientist to pursue it.

Many controversies in science can be viewed as a battle between the opposing biases of conservatism and rebelliousness. According

to **Philip Kitcher**, cognitive variation among scientists on this dimension is conducive to progress in the long run. Some scientists are **mavericks**, quick to challenge established views and pursue new avenues, while others are traditionalists, suspicious of radical ideas and inclined to defend the orthodoxy as long as possible. There is no single strategy that is always successful: the mavericks take more risks and will often turn out to be wrong, but may sometimes strike gold and thus prevent the **ossification** of scientific orthodoxy. Traditionalists are often right in sticking with the old ways, and are not the ones to waste time and effort on wild and improbable ideas. But sometimes they will be proven wrong too.

A desire for fame and success is often viewed as unworthy of a real scientist. The goal of science is truth for its own sake. Although such base motives may indeed compromise one's scientific work, if allowed to be unchecked, there is no convincing reason why they would stand in the way of significant discoveries. Even spite, jealousy, and the desire to humiliate a rival can result in excellent scientific work, if the competing parties know that they have to abide by certain rules, and will be called out whenever they violate them. In any case, a desire for fame and success does not compromise the collective goals of truth and objectivity.

Indeed, social competition may be more effective as an **incentive** to do science than the pure and noble goal of discovery, especially when it comes to the laborious and repetitious work that science often demands. As **Susan Haack** puts it, competition is "an aid to our limited energy and fragile intellectual integrity". **Scooping** a rival may be more thrilling than laying another brick in the edifice of knowledge, but that's no problem, as both may be accomplished at the same time. What goes for individual rivalry also applies to competition between research groups, as David Hull writes: "As unseemly as **factionalism** in science may be, it does serve a positive function. It enlists baser human motives for higher causes".

In all these cases, social influences are not an impediment to the epistemic ambition of science, but rather a facilitator of scientific progress. Science **harnesses** some of the baser motives of human behaviour in the service of truth, making sure that the interplay of

---

Philip Kitcher
菲利普·基切尔（1947— ），英国当代著名科学哲学家，哥伦比亚大学哲学系教授，被美国国家科学教育委员会誉为"达尔文之友"。

maverick
独行其是者；持不同意见者

ossification 僵化

incentive 鼓励；激励

Susan Haack
苏珊·哈克（1945— ），剑桥大学哲学博士，英国分析哲学家，研究逻辑学、认识论和逻辑之法律应用。

scoop 赢得

factionalism
党派之争；党派主义

harness 利用

scientists' individual interests and biases mostly **align with** epistemic progress. Social constructivists are right that, in the battle between competing paradigms (or research programs), the social configuration of the research community plays an important role. This is especially true in the early stages of scientific research, when evidence is still ambiguous and incomplete, conceptual problems abound, and social factors are given free rein. Even the final **vindication** of the correct scientific theory, however, is also accomplished through social means: forming alliances, maintaining a good reputation, showing courage to challenge received views, and exercising restraint in attacking rivals.	align with 与……一致 vindication 证实
Charles Darwin may have been right from the start about the fact of common ancestry, but his theory would not have carried the day as swiftly as it did without Darwin's indefatigable efforts to enlist allies to the cause and to engage and negotiate with his critics. All the parties in the dispute were trying to enlist nature as their ally, but Darwin of course had one big advantage: nature really was on his side all along. In the long run, therefore, as evidence accumulates and **factions** wax and wane, the social influences on science will be filtered out, and rightly so.	faction 派系
(2, 530 words)	

 Recall

Answer the following questions with the information from the passage.

1. In the classical view, why is science free from social influences?
2. According to psychologists, what's the difference between episodic memories and semantic memories?
3. According to Thomas Kuhn, why are the old and the new paradigm "incommensurable"?
4. Concerning the debate about the legacy of Kuhn's work, what's the view of the authors?
5. What do the authors imply by the statement "Isaac Newton was standing on the shoulders of giants"?
6. What do the authors think of the relationship between bias and the progress of science?

II Interpret

Answer the following questions by analysing the passage.

7. At the beginning of Paragraph 17, the authors state, "In general terms, a good social arrangement for finding out the truth of some matter is to have two or more competing groups pursue different hypotheses, trying their utmost to garner evidence for their own view and to prove competitors wrong." Do you agree with this or not? Elaborate your viewpoint.

8. In Paragraph 20, the author says, "Indeed, social competition may be more effective as an incentive to do science than the pure and noble goal of discovery, especially when it comes to the laborious and repetitious work that science often demands." According to the author, what else in science is equally important as social competition?

III Evaluate & Connect

Answer the following question by relating the passage to your own experience.

9. In Paragraph 21, the author says, "In all these cases, social influences are not an impediment to the epistemic ambition of science, but rather a facilitator of scientific progress." Do you think social influences never fail to facilitate scientific progress? Illustrate your viewpoint with personal experience.

Unit 6

Physical Science

Synopsis

  物理学是研究物质最一般的运动规律和物质基本结构的学科。作为自然科学的首要学科，物理学研究大至宇宙，小至基本粒子等一切物质最基本的运动形式和规律，而宇宙大爆炸就是科学家在研究宇宙运动规律中发现的。宇宙中的天体为什么都在离我们而去？原因离不开大爆炸产生的运动。宇宙大爆炸理论的建立是基于两个基本假设：物理定律的普适性和宇宙学原理。大到宇宙的存在和发展，小到生活中的很多方面都和物理学有关系，只有学好物理并且正确运用，才能更好地认识世界和改造世界。本单元 Text A 通过对物理学和宇宙学理论的介绍带领读者深入了解宇宙大爆炸；Text B 介绍了物理学的结构及其原理。

Warm-up

The relationship between matter and various microscopic particles are displayed in the chart below. Read the definitions in the following table first, and then try to label the particles in the picture. Not all the particles in the table are shown in the chart. Do you know anything else about these particles? Share what you know with your partners.

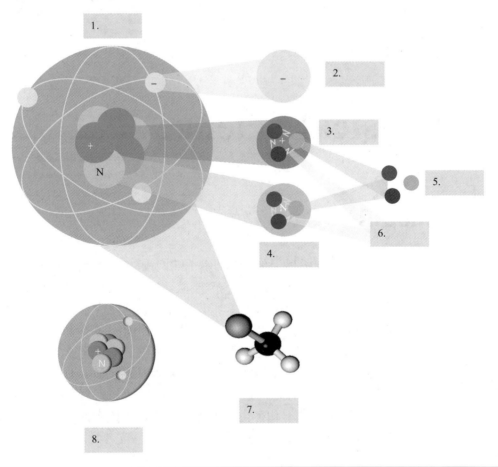

Matter is composed of tiny particles called atoms. Matter takes on different forms depending on how the atoms are arranged.		
Atom	原子	is made up of a nucleus of protons and neutrons and an orbit of electrons that revolve around it.
Electron	电子	is a negatively charged particle. It is the lightest stable subatomic particle known.

Unit 6 Physical Science

(Continued)

Matter is composed of tiny particles called atoms. Matter takes on different forms depending on how the atoms are arranged.		
Proton	质子	is a subatomic particle with positive electric charge much larger than the electron.
Neutron	中子	is a subatomic particle of about the same mass as a proton but without an electric charge.
Quarks	夸克	are the constituents of protons and neutrons.
Hadron	强子	is composed of gluons (胶子), quarks, and anti-quarks.
Bosons	玻色子	are particles that, in some way, transmit the forces of interaction between the rest of the particles.
Molecules	分子	form when two or more atoms form chemical bonds with each other.
Ion	离子	is an atom or group of atoms carrying a positive or negative electric charge as a result of having lost or gained one or more electrons.
Gluon	胶子	is a subatomic particle of a class that is thought to bind quarks together.

Text A

Background information

This article is extracted from the book *A Little History of Science* by William Bynum, which was published by Yale University Press in 2012. The author William Bynum is Emeritus Professor of the History of Medicine, University College London. He is the author and editor of numerous publications, including most recently *Great Discoveries in Medicine*. This book tells the greatest story on earth. From the first scientific discovery to present-day telescopes, the author explains the discoveries and developments that have transformed the world around us and how we understand it. This article explores whether the Big Bang really happened and whether it can explain the universe. It also covers discoveries such as the nebular hypothesis, Einstein's General Theory of Relativity, and Planck's constant, as well as introduces molecular biology and string theory.

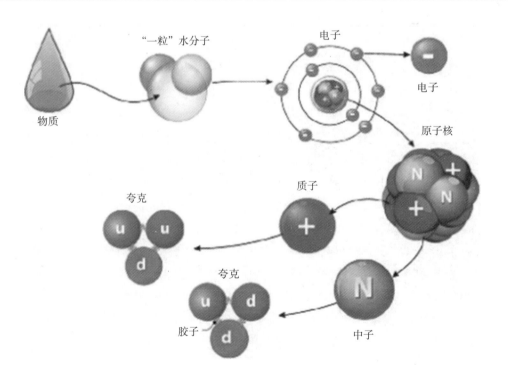

The Big Bang

William Bynum

If a film of the history of the universe had been made, what would happen if you ran it backwards? At about five billion years ago our planet would disappear, for this is when it probably formed, from the **debris** of our solar system. Keep going back to the beginning and what happened then? The Big Bang: an **explosion** so powerful that its temperature and force are still being felt some 13.8 billion years later.

At least this is what scientists from the 1940s began to suggest with increasing confidence. The universe had begun from a point, an unimaginably hot, **dense** state, and then there was the big bang. Ever since this moment, it has been cooling and expanding, carrying the **galaxies** outwards from this original point. Ours is a **dynamic** and exciting universe, in which we are the tiniest of tiny **speck**s. It is composed of the stars, planets and **comet**s making up the visible galaxies; there is also much that's invisible—black holes and the much more abundant "**dark matter**" and 'dark energy'.

So, did the Big Bang really happen, and can it explain the universe? Nobody was there of course, to begin filming. And what happened just before the Big Bang? These are questions that it is impossible to answer with any certainty, but they involve a lot of **cutting-edge physics**, as well as **cosmology** (the study of the universe). They have generated much debate over the past half-century or so. And it goes on right now.

Around 1800, the French **Newtonian**, Laplace, developed his **nebular hypothesis**. He was mainly aiming to argue that the solar system had developed from a giant gas cloud. It convinced a lot of people that the earth had an ancient history, which would help explain its characteristics, such as its central heat, fossils and other **geological** features. Many nineteenth-century scientists passionately disputed the age of the earth and of our galaxy, **the Milky Way**. In the early decades of the twentieth century, two developments radically altered the questions.

---

debris 残骸；碎片
explosion 爆炸

dense 密度大的
galaxy 星系
dynamic 充满活力的
speck 斑点；小点
comet 彗星
dark matter 暗物质

cutting-edge physics 尖端物理学
cosmology 宇宙学

Newtonian 信奉牛顿学说的人
nebular hypothesis 星云假说
geological 地质的
the Milky Way 银河系

The first was Einstein's **General Theory of Relativity**, with its important implications for time and space. By insisting that these two things are intimately related, as '**space-time**', Einstein added a new dimension to the universe. Einstein's mathematical work also implied that space was **curved**, so that **Euclid**'s geometry didn't quite provide an adequate explanation over the vast distances of space. In Euclid's universe, parallel lines go on for ever, and never touch. But this assumes that space is flat. In a flat, Euclidian world, the sum of the angles of a triangle is always 180 degrees. But if you are measuring a triangle on a globe, with its curved surface, this doesn't work. And if space itself is curved, we need different forms of mathematics to deal with it.

Having accepted the essential truth of Einstein's brilliant work, the physicists and cosmologists had some new thinking to do. While the revolution he brought about was largely a theoretical one, the second major development in cosmology was not theoretical. It was based firmly on observations, especially those of the American astronomer **Edwin Hubble** (1889—1953). Hubble was celebrated in 1990 when a space shuttle carried into **orbit** round the earth a space telescope named after him. The Hubble Space Telescope has recently revealed more than even he could have seen with the telescope at the Mount Wilson Observatory in California, where he worked. In the 1920s, Hubble saw further than any astronomer had ever done. He showed that our galaxy (the Milky Way) is not even the beginning of the end of the universe. It is one of countless thousands of other galaxies, stretching even farther than our telescopes can reach.

Cosmologists also remember Hubble for the special number, the "**constant**", attached to his name. (You may remember **Planck's constant**, which was a similar idea.) When light is moving away from us, it shifts the spectrum of its waves to the red end of the visible spectrum. This is called the "**redshift**". If it is moving towards us, its waves shift towards the other end of the spectrum, the "**blueshift**". This is an effect that astronomers can easily measure, and is caused by the same thing that makes trains sound different when they are coming towards you and going away from you. What Hubble saw is that light from very distant stars has red shifts, and the further

General Theory of Relativity 广义相对论，描述物质间引力相互作用的理论。
space-time 时空一体
curved 弯曲的

Euclid
欧几里得（约公元前325—前265），古希腊数学家，被称为"几何之父"。他最著名的著作《几何原本》是欧洲数学的基础。

Edwin Hubble
爱德文·鲍威尔·哈勃，美国著名天文学家，研究现代宇宙理论最著名的人物之一，河外天文学的奠基人和提供宇宙膨胀实例证据的第一人。
orbit
（天体运行的）轨道

Planck's constant
　　普朗克常数，记为h，一个物理常数，用以描述量子大小。马克斯·普朗克发现，只有假定电磁波的发射和吸收不是连续的，而是一份一份地进行的，计算的结果才能和试验结果是相符。这样的一份能量叫做能量子，每一份能量子等于普朗克常数乘以辐射电磁波的频率。

away the star is, the larger the shift. This told him that the stars are moving away from us, and the further away they are, the faster they are moving. The universe is expanding, and it appears to be doing so at an increasing rate. Hubble measured the distance from the stars and the extent of the red shift. His measurements fell on a pretty straight line when he plotted them on a graph. From this he calculated 'Hubble's constant', which he published in a very important paper in 1929. This extraordinary number gave cosmologists a method of calculating the age of the universe.

Hubble's constant has been **refine**d since then. New observations have found stars even farther away, and we can now make more accurate measurements of the red shift. Some of these stars are millions of light years away. A light year is about six trillion earth miles. It takes only eight minutes for a ray of sunlight to reach the earth. If the ray of light then bounced back to the sun, it could make over 32,000 return journeys in a year—another way of trying to appreciate the vast distances involved—and vast amounts of time. Some of what we see in the night sky is light that began its journey a very long time ago from stars that have since become extinct. To get a really precise value for Hubble's constant, we need to know exactly how far away these very distant stars and galaxies are from us. But even with these difficulties, the constant's importance is that it can tell us approximately how long they have been travelling. This gives the age of the universe—beginning with its Big Bang.

The Big Bang was popularised in the 1940s by **George Gamow** (1904—1968). Gamow was a colourful Russian-born physicist who went to America in the early 1930s. He had a wonderfully creative mind, contributing ideas to **molecular biology** as well as physics and relativity theory. With a colleague, he explored, at the micro level, how the nucleus of an atom emits electrons (beta particles). On the **grand scale**, he looked at how **nebulae**—massive clouds of hot particles and cosmic dust—are formed. His theory of the Big Bang, worked out from 1948 with others, built on knowledge of the smallest constituents of atoms, combined with a model of what might have happened when the universe began.

redshift
红移，指物体的电磁辐射由于某种原因导致波长增加、频率降低的现象。在可见光波段，表现为光谱的谱线向红色端移动。

blueshift
蓝移，指电磁辐射由于某种原因导致波长变短、频率升高的现象，在可见光波段，表现为光谱的谱线朝蓝端移动了一段距离。

refine 改进；改善

George Gamow
乔治·伽莫夫，宇宙大爆炸理论奠基人。

molecular biology 分子生物学
grand scale 大规模
nebulae 星云

First, **the constituents: the particles and forces**. In the late 1940s this bit of physics came to be called **quantum electrodynamics** or QED for short. One man who helped make sense of it was the American physicist **Richard Feynman** (1918—1988). He is famous for the diagrams he drew (sometimes on restaurant napkins) to explain his theories and his mathematics, and for playing the **bongo drums**. He won the Nobel Prize in 1965, primarily for his work on QED, which provided the complicated mathematics to describe the even smaller particles and forces that we examine below.

After the end of the Second World War, particle physicists continued to accelerate atoms and then particles in increasingly more powerful particle **accelerator**s. The accelerators can break up atoms into their sub-atomic particles, which is like reversing what might have happened a few instants after the Big Bang. Immediately after the Big Bang, as cooling began, the building-blocks of matter would have begun to form. From the particles would come the atoms and from the atoms the elements, and so on up to the planets and stars.

As Einstein's $E = mc^2$ tells us, at ever-higher speeds—almost the speed of light—in the accelerators, the mass is mostly converted into energy. The physicists found that these very fast particles do some fascinating things. The electron emerges unchanged from the accelerator. It is part of a family of force-particles—the **leptons**. The proton and neutron turn out to be composed of even smaller particles called *quarks*. There are several kinds. Each comes with a charge. Combined into threes, they make up a neutron or a proton.

There are four basic forces in the universe. Understanding how they relate to each other has been one of the great quests of the twentieth century. Gravity is the weakest, but acts at an infinite distance. It is still not entirely understood, even though we have been officially puzzling about it since Newton's apple. **Electromagnetism** is involved in many aspects of nature. It keeps the electrons in their orbits in the atom, and, as light, brings us daily news that the sun is still shining. Also in the atom are the strong and weak nuclear forces. These two bind the particles within the nucleus of the atom.

Leaving aside gravity, the other forces work by the exchange of special particles—force carriers—called bosons. These include the **photon**, Einstein's quantum of light, which is the boson for electromagnetism. Yet, perhaps the most famous boson is the missing one: **the Higgs Boson**. Particle physicists have been looking it for since the 1960s. This boson is thought to create mass in other particles. Finding it would help explain how particles gained their mass in the immediate aftermath of the Big Bang. At the world's biggest particle accelerator, **the Large Hadron Collider** (LHC) near Geneva, Switzerland, scientists think they caught a glimpse of it on their instruments in 2012. The LHC was constructed between 1998 and 2008 by the European Organisation for Nuclear Research (CERN). CERN itself was established in 1954. It was a cooperative scientific enterprise among several European countries, a result of the high cost of physics research, and the need for many scientists, technicians and computer staff to perform and interpret these experiments at the **extreme**s of matter and energy.

The Higgs Boson would be an extremely useful (but not the final) part of the puzzle known as the Standard Model, which accounts for everything except gravity. And a confirmed Standard Model would move close to a "Theory of Everything", possibly via string theory, an approach to analysing all these forces and particles. **String theory** is based on the assumption that these fundamental forces of nature can be considered as if they were one-dimensional vibrating strings. It uses very complicated mathematics. This work is still science in the making.

A lot of this micro-level particle physics is difficult to associate with the ordinary world we live in. But scientists are finding more and more uses for it in nuclear energy, television, computers, quantum computing and medical screening equipment. Beyond these important uses in our daily lives, there is much to be learned too as the idea of the Big Bang has been fitted into what can be seen and not seen in the far reaches of space.

photon 光子，是传递电磁相互作用的基本粒子，是一种规范玻色子。

the Higgs Boson
希格斯玻色子，于2012年在欧洲核子研究中心（CERN）的大型强子对撞机（LHC）上被发现。它的发现是粒子物理学中的一个重大突破，因为它证实了希格斯机制的存在，并填补了标准模型（Standard Model）中最后一个缺失的环节。

the Large Hadron Collider
大型强子对撞机

extreme 极端，极限

String theory
弦理论是理论物理的一个分支学科；它的一个基本观点是，自然界的基本单元不是电子、光子、中微子和夸克之类的点状粒子，而是很小的、线状的"弦"。弦的不同振动和运动就产生出各种不同的基本粒子。

In the 1920s, the Russian physicist **Alexander Friedman** (1888—1925) was one of those who quickly **assimilate**d Einstein's general theory of relativity into his own mathematical understanding of the universe. His Friedman Equations provided rules for an expanding universe. Friedman also wondered if it mattered that we looked out at the stars from earth. It's a special place for us, but did this give us a unique place for seeing the universe? He said no, it didn't matter. It's just where we happen to be. Things would not look different if we were on some other planet, light years away. This is Friedman's Cosmological Constant. It gives us another important idea: that matter is uniformly distributed throughout the universe. There are local variations, of course—the earth is much denser than the surrounding atmosphere. But smoothed out across all space, the principle appears to be true. Today, cosmologists still base much of their exploration on Friedman's models. They also have to deal with mysterious things such as black holes and dark matter.

Two fellows of the Royal Society discussed the idea of a 'dark star' in the eighteenth century. Describing its modern equivalent, the 'black hole', was the work of a modern mathematical genius, Roger Penrose (b. 1931), and a brilliant theoretical physicist, **Stephen Hawking** (1942—2018). Until his retirement, Hawking had Isaac Newton's old job as Lucasian Professor of Mathematics at the University of Cambridge. Together they explained how black holes are easy to imagine, but of course impossible to see. This is because they are caused by areas in space where dying stars have gradually shrunk. As their remaining matter becomes more densely packed, the forces of gravity become so strong that the photons of light are trapped and cannot get out.

There are also super-massive black holes. In 2008 the Milky Way's very own super black hole—**Sagittarius A***—was confirmed after a sixteen-year hunt with telescopes in Chile. Astronomers led by the German **Reinhard Genzel** (b. 1952) watched the patterns of the stars that orbit the black hole at the centre of the galaxy. They used measurements of infra-red light because there is so much **stellar** dust between the black hole and us, 27,000 light years away.

These super-massive black holes might play a part in the formation

Alexander Friedman
亚历山大·弗里德曼（1888—1925），俄罗斯数学家和物理学家，他最重要的工作是提出了第一个基于爱因斯坦广义相对论的宇宙模型，即弗里德曼−勒梅特−罗伯逊−沃尔克度规（Friedmann-Lemaître-Robertson-Walker metric）。

assimilate 同化，吸收

Stephen Hawking
斯蒂芬·霍金（1942—2018），理论物物理学家，宇宙学家，科学思想家。

Sagittarius A*
人马座 A*（简写为 Sgr A*，星号 * 读作"star"）是位于银河系银心一个非常光亮及致密的射电波源，是离我们最近的超大质量黑洞的所在。

Reinhard Genzel
赖因哈德·根策尔

of galaxies and involve another part of space we cannot see directly: dark matter. Dark matter is thought to account for much more of the universe—80% of its matter—than the 4% of the visible stars and planets together with gas and space dust. Dark matter was first considered in the 1930s, to explain why large bits of the universe did not behave exactly as predicted. Scientists had realised there was a mismatch between the mass of the visible parts and their gravitational effects: something was missing. In the 1970s, the astronomer Vera Rubin (1928—2016) charted how fast stars on the edge of galaxies were moving. They were travelling faster than they should have been. Traditionally it was thought that the further they were away from the centre of the galaxy, the slower they would orbit. Dark matter would provide the extra gravity needed to speed up the stars. So indirectly evidence of dark matter was provided and it has been generally accepted. But what dark matter is remains a mystery—something else to be found or **disprove**d in the future.

Modern cosmology has emerged from Einstein's theories, from thousands upon thousands of observations, with computers to analyse the data, and from Gamow's idea of the Big Bang. Like any good theory in science, the Big Bang has changed since Gamow's time. In fact, for two decades after it was put forward in 1948, physicists hardly concerned themselves with the origins of the universe. The Big Bang had to contend with another model of the universe, called the '**steady state**' one, most associated with the astronomer **Fred Hoyle** (1915—2001). Hoyle's model enjoyed some backing in the 1950s. It suggested an infinite universe, with the continuous creation of new matter. In this mode, the universe has no beginning and no end. There were so many difficulties with the steady-state idea that it had only a brief scientific life.

Physicists now have information about short-lived particles and forces gathered in particle accelerators. They have observations in the far reaches of space. They have been able to refine what we know about the Big Bang. There is still a lot of disagreement about details, and even about some of the fundamental principles, but this is not unusual in science. The Big Bang model can make sense of much that can now be measured, including the red shifts of distant stars,

（1952— ），现任慕尼黑马克斯-普朗克太空物理学研究所所长，因在银河系中央发现超大质量天体获得2020年诺贝尔物理学奖。

stellar 恒星的

disprove 证明……是错误的

steady state 恒定状态

Fred Hoyle

弗雷德·霍伊尔（1915—2001），英国著名天文学家，因对宇宙学上长期占统治地位的大爆炸理论的挑战而闻名。

background cosmic radiation and the fundamental atomic forces. It can accommodate black holes and dark matter. What the model does not do, is say *why* the Big Bang happened. But, then, science deals with the how, not the why. As in all branches of science, some physicists and cosmologists have religious beliefs and others do not. That is how it should be. The best science is done in an atmosphere of tolerance.

(2, 717 words)

❶ Recall

Answer the following questions with the information from the passage.

1. What is the Big Bang?
2. What radically altered scientists' idea of the age of Earth and the Milky Way in the early decades of the 20th century?
3. Who popularised the Big Bang in the 1940s? What was his theory of the Big Bang build on?
4. What has been one of the great quests of the 20th century?
5. Why couldn't the Higgs Boson theory solve the puzzle known as the Standard Model?
6. Why are black holes easy to imagine but impossible to see?

❷ Interpret

Answer the following question by analysing the passage.

7. In Paragraph 3 from the bottom, the writer mentions, "Scientists had realised there was a mismatch between the mass of the visible parts and their gravitational effects." How did they find this mismatch? According to the text, what is the universe composed of?

❸ Evaluate & Connect

Answer the following questions by relating the passage to your own experience.

8. In paragraph 16, there is the statement "A lot of this micro-level particle physics is difficult to associate with the ordinary world we live in. But scientists are finding more and more uses for it in nuclear energy, television, computers, quantum computing and medical screening equipment." Based on this text and your own knowledge, make some comments on how micro-level particle physics influences the ordinary world we live in.
9. The last sentence of Text A is "The best science is done in an atmosphere of tolerance." Based on Text A and your own knowledge, make some comments on this sentence. Is it also true for ancient Chinese physics?

Text B

Background Information

This article is extracted from the book *Teach Yourself Physics* (a travel companion) by Jakob Schwichtenberg. The author includes many suggestions and recommendations on learning physics, and more importantly, gives a clear map of physics. The goal of this book is to encourage more people to think deeply about nature by using the appropriate tools, and to implant a new way of thinking. This article belongs to the second part of the book and is followed by a subjects guide. It starts with a bird's eye view of physics and then introduces the structure of physics as a discipline.

The Structure of Physics

Jakob Schwichtenberg

In a nutshell, physics can be summarized as follows. We take **a chunk of** reality that we want to understand and translate it into mathematics. More specifically, this means that we **encode** our findings in the form of **equation**s. Using these equations, we can make predictions and test our ideas.

Formulated differently, our goal in physics is to describe, understand, and explain what is going on in nature.

There are, of course, lots of scientific **discipline**s which try to make sense of nature. So how does physics fit into the bigger picture? One answer to this question can be illustrated this way:

In words, this means that in physics we try to describe nature at the largest (planets, galaxies, the universe) and smallest scales (**elementary** particles). But these are only the **grandest** of goals. We can also use our physics toolbox to make sense of, say, everyday objects or **electromagnetic** waves. The thing is, there is not only a **hierarchy** of different scientific disciplines, but also a hierarchy within physics. This is something we will talk about in a moment. But

a chunk of 大块；相当大的量	
encode 编码	
equation 方程式；等式	
formulate 阐述	
discipline 知识领域	
elementary 基本的	
grandest 宏大的	
electromagnetic 电磁的	
hierarchy 层次体系	

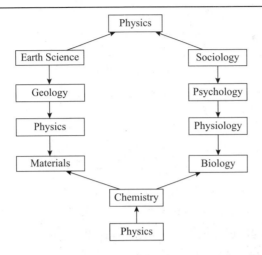

first, we need to talk about what it is that we do in physics or, more commonly, try to do.

First of all, of course, we observe. Then, as soon as we have found some phenomena or class of phenomena we want to describe, we can start "doing physics". Our task is to find suitable **handle**s onto the world. In physics, usually we call these handles "**degrees of freedom**". Examples are the position and **momentum** of a particle, the frequency and **amplitude** of an **oscillator**, or the temperature and pressure of a gas.

Next, we try to come up with experimental **setup**s which allow us to isolate individual degrees of freedom as much as possible. In other words, we **shield** a specific tiny part of the universe (our subsystem/our experiment) from irrelevant degrees of freedom, so that we can investigate the degrees of freedom we are interested in. Then, to learn something about Nature, we "**poke** it". In concrete terms, this means that we shake our handles and observe how they react. Martin H. Krieger describes it poetically:

"One needs to shake the handle with just the right energy, and in just the right direction, and one will hear the music of Nature in its purest forms."

We then try to describe what we observe by writing down a "model". A model consists of **formula**s that relate the mathematical objects representing our degrees of freedom.

handle 手柄，媒介
degrees of freedom 自由度
momentum 动量
amplitude 振幅
oscillator 振荡器
setup 装置
shield 给……加防护罩

poke 捅；戳

formula 公式；方案

After some time, there will be a large collection of models describing all kinds of phenomena related to several specific degrees of freedom. This is usually the time for a huge step forward. Someone has to come up with something that allows us to see the forest and not just the trees. In other words, the goal is now to find a "theory" that allows us to understand all these models in a common context.

After a theory has been proposed, it must be tested in experiments. **Crucially**, it is not enough that the theory allows us to understand all relevant known phenomena, but it must also predict things we didn't see previously. A good theory makes predictions not only postdictions. The symbiotic relationship between experiments and theoretical ideas is one of the **hallmark**s of physics. In the words, of Richard Feynman:

> "It doesn't matter how beautiful your theory is, it doesn't matter how smart you are. If it doesn't agree with experiment, it's wrong."

Often, theoretical ideas are **inspire**d by experimental observations. In turn, theoretical ideas inspire new experiments which then lead to new theoretical ideas and so on.

For example, physicists used collider experiments to investigate the properties of elementary particles like **quarks, photons, and electrons**. The behaviour and **interplay** of these particles can be described using models like **Quantum Electrodynamics and Quantum Chromodynamics**. Both are models in the framework of quantum field theory. And in turn, physicists used quantum field theory to propose new models like the **Electroweak Model** which was confirmed experimentally through the discovery of the Higgs particle.

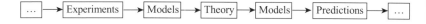

This is a bird's eye view of physics, then how about the internal structure of physics and especially the relationship between theories and models in a bit more detail?

In physics, there isn't one universally applicable theory. Each theory has specific strengths and weaknesses. Which theory we use always depends on the system at hand. This can be quite confusing, especially for beginning students. Many first-year students are frustrated why they have to learn an "outdated" theory like classical mechanics. Everyone knows that classical mechanics has been replaced with quantum mechanics, right?

Actually, that's not correct. Classical mechanics is still the best theory of everyday objects that we have. Quantum mechanics does not help us in any way to describe how, say, a ball rolls down a ramp. But quantum mechanics is, of course, perfectly suited for other systems, like the **hydrogen atom** where classical mechanics fails horribly.

hydrogen atom 氢原子

In concrete terms, (oversimplifying a bit):

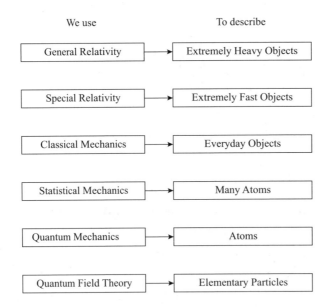

While this way of looking at the structure of physics can be helpful, there are also other ways of looking at it. For example, the following table summarizes the role of the most important physical theories and models a bit more systematically.

Whenever you feel lost while studying physics, you should come back here and see how exactly what you're learning fits into the bigger picture.

Now, let's talk about the relationship between the various theories. This can be understood nicely using an illustration known as "the cube of physics".

Theory	Model	Application	Example
Classical Field Theory	General Relativity	Cosimology	Black Holes
Classical Mechanics	Electrodynamics	Optics, Electrical Engineering	Free Electromagnetic Waves
Quantum Mechanics	Special Relativity	Engineering	Length Contraction of a Moving Stick
Quantum Field Theory	Newtonian Mechanics	Engineering	Ball Rolling Down a Ramp
	Statistical Mechanics	Thermodynamics	Ideal Gas
	Non-Relativistic Quantum Mechanics	Atomic Physics	Hydrogen Atom
	Relativistic Quantum Mechanics	Atomic Physics	Thomas precession
	QED, QCD, Standard Model	Particle Physics	Bhabha Scottering
	Ising Model, Ginzburg-Landau model	Solid State Physics	Feromagnet, Supercondutors

The Cube of physics

The cube of physics is a map which helps us to **navigate** the landscape of physical theories. The main idea is to make sense of this landscape by talking about the following fundamental **constant**s:

navigate 导航；探索

constant 常数

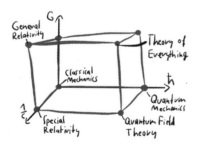

➤ The speed of light c = 2.997,9 × 10^8 m/s, which encodes **an upper speed limit for all physical processes**.

➤ The gravitational constant G = 6.674,1 × 10^{-11}, which encodes **the strength of gravitational interactions**.

➤ The (reduced) Planck constant $\hbar$ = 1.054,57 × 10^{-34}, which encodes **the magnitude of quantum effects**.

While these are, well, constants, we imagine what happens when we vary them. This is motivated by the observation that when every object in a given system moves extremely slowly compared to the speed of light ($v \ll c$), we can act as if c → ∞ to simplify our

an upper speed limit for all physical processes
　所有物理进程的速度上限

the strength of gravitational interactions
　引力相互作用的强度

the magnitude of quantum effects
　量子效应的大小

equations. As mentioned above, the speed of light is an upper speed limit. No object can move with a **velocity** faster than c. So taking c → ∞ corresponds to a situation in which there is no such speed limit at all. While there is *always* this speed limit in physics, we can act as if there were none if we only consider slowly moving objects.

| | velocity 速度 |

Just imagine there was a highway with an upper speed limit of v_{max} = 100,000,000km/h while no car can drive faster than v ≈ 300km/h. So technically there is a speed limit, but it doesn't matter, and we can act as if there was none.

Similarly, by considering the limit G → 0, we end up with theories in which there is no gravity at all. And by considering the limit h → 0, we end up with a theory in which quantum effects play no role.

So the most accurate theory of physics takes the upper speed limit (c≠∞), gravitational interactions (G≠0) and quantum effects (h≠0) into account. This would be a **theory of everything** and, so far, no one has succeeded in writing it down.

| | Theory of Everything 万物理论 |

While this is certainly a big problem, it doesn't stop us from making astonishingly accurate predictions. Depending on the system at hand, we can act as if certain effects don't exist at all. And this is how we end up with the various theories which live at the corner points of the cube of physics:

➢ Whenever it is reasonable to ignore gravitational interactions G → 0 (e.g., for elementary particles), we can use **quantum field theory**.

| | Quantum Field Theory 量子场理论 |

➢ For systems in which it is reasonable to ignore quantum effects h → 0 (e.g., planets), we can use **general relativity**.

| | General Relativity 广义相对论 |

If we can ignore quantum effects *and* gravitational interactions (h → 0 and G → 0), we can use **special relativity**.

| | Special Relativity 狭义相对论 |

➢ Moreover, when it is reasonable to ignore gravitational interactions and that there is an upper speed limit (G → 0 and $\frac{1}{c}$ → 0), we can use **quantum mechanics**.

| | Quantum Mechanics 量子力学 |

➢ For systems in which we can ignore quantum effects and that there is an upper speed limit (h → 0 and $\frac{1}{c}$ → 0), we can use classical mechanics with Newton's laws to describe gravity. (The resulting model is often called Newtonian gravity.)

➤ And finally, if we can ignore quantum effects, the upper speed limit, *and* gravitational interactions ($h \to 0$, $\frac{1}{c} \to 0$ and $G \to 0$), we can use non-relativistic classical mechanics without gravity.

If you still find the cube of physics confusing, here's an **alternative** perspective:

alternative 可供替代的

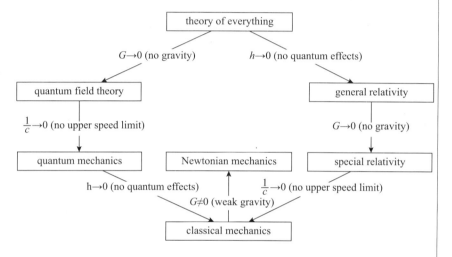

You still may wonder why people still care so much about "outdated" theories like classical mechanics. So, let's talk about this next.

Why physics works

Why do we still talk about classical mechanics if we know about quantum mechanics? Why is classical electrodynamics still relevant if we know about **quantum electrodynamics**? And why do people even talk about chemistry, biology, and economics if it all **boils down** to physics on a fundamental level?

quantum electrodynamics 量子电动力学

boil down 总结

A pragmatic answer would be that older theories like classical mechanics or electrodynamics are necessary **prerequisite**s for all the new stuff. Students are often told that they need to master classical mechanics before they can even hope to develop any understanding of quantum mechanics.

prerequisite 前提条件

I personally think this is nonsense. Quantum mechanics and quantum field theory aren't **intrinsically** more complicated than

intrinsically 本质上

our classical theories. All theories can be extremely simple or complicated, depending on the model and application at hand. But this is not really the point I want to make here.

Instead, the real reason why fundamental physics hasn't taken over the world is that phenomena on different scales are usually **decouple**d from each other.

Let's say, for example, that we want to describe a **pendulum**. The basic quantities that are relevant to describe a pendulum are its period w, its mass m, its length l and the acceleration g any object feels in the earth's gravitational field. A typical task in physics is now to predict the **period** w of a specific pendulum.

To solve this problem, we first note that a period is measured in seconds, a mass in kilograms, a length in meters and an **acceleration** in meter per second squared. Moreover, we want a formula with the period w on one side of the equation:

$$w = \underline{\qquad} \;?$$

Since a period is measured in seconds, the right-hand side of the formula must be measured in seconds too. Otherwise, we would be comparing apples to oranges. If we look at the basic quantities listed above, we discover that if we divide a length (measured in meters) by an acceleration (measured in meters per second squared), we get something with units second squared:

$$\text{units of } \frac{l}{g} = \frac{meters}{\frac{meters}{seconds^2}} = seconds^2$$

Therefore, the square root of this **fraction** is measured in seconds and is therefore an ideal candidate for the right-hand side of Eq. 1:

$$w = c\sqrt{\frac{l}{g}}$$

where C denotes some dimensionless constant. This equation works remarkably well.[1]

What we have discovered here is that the period of a pendulum is independent of its mass and can be predicted once its length l is known. All of this is completely independent of the pendulum's

decouple 分离；解耦

pendulum 钟摆

period 周期

acceleration 加速度

fraction 分数

---

1 As long as the pendulum only swings a little, this equation works perfectly. For larger oscillations, further correction terms are needed.

microstructural constitution. We used absolutely no details about the pendulum in the **derivation** above and the equation works for all kinds of pendulums, **irrespective** of what they are made of.

A pendulum consists of atoms which, in turn, consist of electrons and quarks. The behaviour of quarks and electrons can be described using quantum field theory. But as we've just seen, such details are completely irrelevant for our description of a pendulum.

We could, of course, try to build a model of a pendulum that takes the positions, **momenta**, and interactions of the billions of electrons and quarks that our pendulum consists of into account. But such a project is not only deemed to fail but is also completely **futile**. A model of a pendulum that "employed all known physics fully" would also include the standard model, general relativity, and quantum contributions. So, it would be too complex to give us any results. Therefore, any question we may have about a pendulum, can be answered perfectly using much simpler equations such as Eq. 3.

Also, a system that consists of so many "more fundamental" building blocks can exhibit features which simply don't exist if we only consider one or a few of the building blocks in isolation. This is known as emergence.

To illustrate this, just think about a traffic jam. A traffic jam consists of lots of cars. And cars consist of lots of individual components that consist of atoms that consist of quarks and electrons. But studying these individual components, atoms, or even quarks and electrons is not helpful if we want to understand traffic jams.

Similarly, knowing the laws of quantum field theory does not help us describe the stock market, even though humans consist of quarks and electrons, too.

Using the language introduced in the previous part, we can summarize that descriptions on different scales require different handles. A description on a **microscopic** level must formulate its laws in terms of positions and momenta of individual elementary particles. But a description of a pendulum on **macroscopic** scales works perfectly well if it uses handles like its period. In between—on mesoscopic scales—even different handles may be more helpful, as demonstrated perfectly by disciplines like chemistry and biology.

---

microstructural constitution 显微结构构成

derivation 推导

irrespective 无关的

momenta 动量；动力

futile 无效的；徒劳的

microscopic 微小的

macroscopic 宏观的；肉眼可见的

The fundamental reason for this phenomenon, known as emergence, is that details become less relevant when we **zoom out**. Furthermore, completely new patterns can emerge, depending on how far we zoom in.

zoom out 调整焦距因此图像更小也更远；广角

This observation is, in some sense, like a Declaration of Independence for different disciplines from each other.

In fact, it would be impossible to do physics if systems at classical scales didn't decouple from those at quantum gravitational scales. Just imagine needing quantum gravity—a theory we know nothing about as of yet—to talk about a baseball's **trajectory**.

trajectory 轨迹

We couldn't make any predictions if microscopic details wouldn't decouple from our macroscopic world since even our best theories of fundamental physics are quite likely not the end of the story. It would be **astounding** if our somewhat naive pictures of spacetime and elementary particles would continue to make sense at **arbitrarily** small scales. Every time physicists successfully "zoomed deeper in" a whole new world opened up. First quantum mechanics, then quantum field theory; and who knows what will come next.

astounding 令人震惊的

arbitrarily 任意地

The reason that we can use the models and theories that we currently have to make astonishingly accurate predictions is that they are independent of whatever happens at much smaller scales. We say the patterns that we observe at a given scale emerge from the microscopic substructure. And most importantly, the features of the handles that we use at a given scale are **robust** and do not depend on microscopic details. Otherwise, they would be quite useless.

robust 强健的，富有活力的

Just as it would be impossible to make predictions about a baseball if its behaviour depends on the exact behaviour of all the atoms it consists of, it would also be impossible to describe electrons and quarks accurately if they depend on the exact behaviour of whatever more fundamental stuff exists at even tinier scales.

In technical terms, we say that our theories are "effective theories" that are perfectly valid descriptions at a given scale. At some point, if we zoom in or out, our effective description becomes invalid or useless and must be replaced by a new effective description.[1]

So the key message to take away is that the various models and theories that have proven to be highly successful in the past will continue to be useful. New theories rarely replace existing ones but merely allow a description on different scales.

Formulations and Interpretations

One thing which can make physics confusing is that there are not just different theories that we need to use at different scales, but also different ways of how we can use a given theory to describe a system.

This is possible because there are different mathematical **arenas** we can use as the stage on which physics happens. The simplest example is a straight-forward **abstraction** of the physical space we live in. But there are also more abstract ones like **configuration space, phase space, and Hilbert space**. Each of these mathematical arenas has particular advantages and, once more, it depends on the system at hand which one we use.

For example, typically quantum mechanics is formulated in Hilbert space. But it is equally possible to formulate it in phase space, configuration space or even physical space. In general, we call the description of a given theory in a particular mathematical arena a formulation of the theory. So in other words, there are always different formulations of each theory. This is similar to how you can describe the number 1,021 using the English word "one thousand twenty-one", using the German word "Eintausend Einundzwanzig", "MXXI" in Roman numerals, or "1111111101" in the **binary** number system. Each of these descriptions has particular advantages depending on the context.

The following table summarizes the names of the most famous formulations of our theories:

arenas 圆形运动场，竞技场

abstraction 抽象化

configuration space, phase space, and Hilbert space
位形空间、相空间和希尔伯特空间

binary 两分的

---

[1] The mathematical tool that allows us to relate effective descriptions that are valid on different scales is known as the renormalization group.

Theory Arena	Everyday Space	Configuration Space	Phase Space	Hilbert Space
Classical Field Theory	Standard Formulation	Lagrangian Formulation	Hamiltonian Formulation	
Classical Mechanics	Newtonian Formulation			Koopman-von Neumann Formulation
Quantum Mechanics	Pilot-Wave Formulation	Path-Integral Formulation	Phase-Space Formulation	Wave-Function Formulation
Quantum Field Theory				Canonical Formulation

Disclaimer: Take note that the name "Standard Formulation" is not a term people really use. There is no standard name for the physical space formulation of classical field theory. If we simply say classical field theory or use a particular model like electrodynamics, we automatically mean the formulation in physical space. Only the formulations in more abstract spaces have a special name. Also take note that there are two empty spots which means that either these formulations have not been worked out yet or they are extremely well hidden in physics literature. Lastly take note that the **pilot-wave formulation** of quantum field theory has not been fully worked out yet and is not generally accepted as satisfactory.

A second crucial thing to understand is that in addition to these various formulations there are also different interpretations of the various theories. This is something people can get really passionate about. While no one is questioning the validity of the different formulations listed above, as they can be shown to be mathematically equivalent, people love to argue about the **pros and cons** of their favourite interpretations. This is especially true in the context of general relativity and quantum mechanics.

pilot-wave formulation 导波公式

pros and cons 利弊

Unfortunately, people often fail to keep the notions "theory", "model", and "interpretation" sufficiently separate. And this is something which can quickly lead to a lot of confusion.

There is one more thing I want to mention. The main reason that physics often appears so **intimidating** is that applications of any theory quickly become extremely complicated. The key here is to recognize that it's only the applications which are difficult, and not the theory itself. So, whenever you feel lost, try to focus on the fundamentals. This way you can always get 80% of the benefits without struggling for months trying to understand confusing mathematical **machinery**.

At this point it is hopefully clear that physics has an incredibly rich menu to offer and no single person can master it all. Nevertheless, it is possible to develop a deep understanding of how nature works at fundamental levels in a relatively short period of time. The key is, of course, to focus on the right things.

(3, 302 words)

intimidating 令人胆怯的

machinery 系统；机械装置

❶ Recall

Answer the following questions with the information from the passage.

1. What is the goal in physics?
2. What steps are taken to achieve that goal?
3. What constants are mentioned in the article?
4. Under what circumstances can we use classical mechanics with Newton's law to describe gravity?
5. What can make physics confusing according to the text?

❷ Interpret

Answer the following question by analysing the passage.

6. According to the author, why do we still talk about classical mechanics if we now know about quantum mechanics?

Ⅲ Evaluate & Connect

Answer the following questions by relating the passage to your own experience.

7. What do you think of the Theory of Everything? Do you think there is a theory/ instrument/ medicine for everything?

8. If you had to do a research on microbes (微生物), what could you do to observe it?

Unit 7

Life Science

Synopsis

人类的祖先在哪里？人类又是如何进化而来的？这些问题一直困扰着努力探索人类进化奥秘的人们。英国 19 世纪著名生物学家查尔斯·达尔文一生致力于揭秘人类起源的真相。在 1859 年出版的《物种起源》中，达尔文提出生物进化论，强调适者生存。在 1871 年出版的《人类的起源》中，达尔文假设我们的祖先来自非洲，非洲类人猿与人类最为相似，但却没有化石证据。本单元 Text A 通过深入探讨人类的生物适应性，激发读者思考人类进化过程中身体结构和行为差异与不同环境适应性之间的关系；Text B 通过说明南非"汤村儿童"头骨化石与英国"皮尔丹人"头骨化石以及研究古人 DNA 对追溯人类起源的影响，向读者揭示人类起源奥秘的复杂性。

Warm-up

Charles Darwin (1809—1882), the well-known British scientist, laid the foundation of modern evolutionary theory with his theory on the development of all life forms through the slow-working process of natural selection. He exerted a major influence on the life and earth sciences and on modern thought in general. He published his theory of evolution with compelling evidence in his 1859 book *On the Origin of Species*. What else do you know about Darwinian theory of evolution?

Below are six concepts that may help you explain Darwinian theory of evolution. Can you explain them in your own words?

(1) variation (2) inheritance (3) over-reproduction

(4) competition (5) adaptation (6) selection and survival

Text A

Background Information

The text is excerpted from the article "Human Biological Adaptability" published in *Science* in 1969 by the American Association for the Advancement of Science. The Author Gabriel W. Lasker (April 29, 1912—August 27, 2002) was a British-born American biological anthropologist. Lasker received the Charles R. Darwin Lifetime Achievement Award in 1993 and the Franz Boas Distinguished Achievement Award from the American Association for the Advancement of Science in 1996. In 1974, he founded the Human Biology Council (later renamed Human Biology Association) to support the publication of *Human Biology*. In 2005, the American Association of Physical Anthropologists established the Gabriel W. Lasker Service Award in his honour.

Human Biological Adaptability

Gabriel W. Lasker

Adaptation is the change by which organisms **surmount** the challenges to life. In the broadest sense, biological adaptation encompasses every necessary biological process: biochemical, physiological, and genetic. Human adaptation covers both functional processes and the structures on which they depend. It differs from human biology as a whole chiefly by its limitation to the concern with how the organism relates to the circumstances it must meet to live.

Adaptation implies its **antithesis**: if one way of functioning is adaptive, another is less adaptive or disadaptive under comparable circumstances. From this springs the idea of adaptive selection, the central theme of the Darwinian theory of evolution—the natural selection of better-adapted organisms and the extinction of the less well adapted through reduced **fertility** or earlier death. In this sense adaptation is a modification in structure or function that enables an organism to survive and reproduce. The term can apply to a

---

surmount 克服；超越

antithesis 对立面

fertility 繁殖力

particular organ or the whole individual and to entire populations or whole species. The more different the individuals or species are, the more able we are to identify the relation of the **anatomical** differences to different behaviour and different adaptation to the environment. Adaptation occurs at three levels: (i) selection of **genotype**, (ii) **ontogenetic** modification, and (iii) physiological and behavioural response. As one goes from inter-specific differences to individual differences within the human species, the chief emphasis shifts from the first level to the second and third. This can be exemplified by anthropological studies of human adaptation to altitude, cold, heat, and other circumstances.

Altitude adaptation

Adaptation of man to high altitudes involves numerically a relatively small problem. Only about 25 million people of the world's people live in high mountains. But high altitudes, with their low atmospheric oxygen tension, present an environmental problem that could not be modified by human inventions until the present century when bottled oxygen and other such therapies were available for treating mountain sickness. Men living in the mountains use drugs such as alcohol and coca to lessen their psychological burden, and this may alter the nature of their response and hence the impact of the conditions. However, the extent to which these drugs **ameliorate** the physiological burden of the altitude seems to be slight although consumption of alcohol can raise the foot temperature of the highland Indian and increase his comfort during the cold of night.

When individuals climb from sea level to an elevation of 4,000 meters or more, there are large differences in the extent of the response and some individuals may even die of **pulmonary oedema**. However, a usual response is an increased rate of breathing and an increased pulse rate under comparable workloads. After a few days at that altitude there is some short-run "adaptation," including increase in **haemoglobin** concentrations, but there still are difficulties in working. Families who continue to live there incur increased risks of **miscarriages**, birth defects, and infant deaths. Individuals reared at these elevations achieve more adequate

Sidebar:
anatomical 身体结构上的

genotype 基因型

ontogenetic 个体发育的

ameliorate 减轻

pulmonary oedema 肺水肿

haemoglobin 血红蛋白

miscarriage 流产

adaptation and the risks are lower. Those born into populations genetically adapted to the altitude apparently do better still. Newman and Collazos and, more recently, Baker report that in the **Peruvian Andes** growth and skeletal maturation is retarded; the consequent relative stunting is possibly an advantage. Chest measurements do not follow this trend toward small dimensions, however; Indian boys in the high mountains of Peru, while developing more slowly than coastal dwellers in other respects, develop a larger **thorax** and greater lung capacity.

Mountain dwellers thus show the three chief **modalities** of adaptation: (i) short-run physiological changes; (ii) modifications during growth and development; and (iii) modification of the gene pool of the population. It is probable that the well-adapted mountain dweller suffers some relative shortcomings when at sea level, but since the Indians who migrate from the Andes to the cities on the coast suffer some of the same kinds of social disabilities as **Appalachian Mountain** folk do in the core cities of the United States, analysis of purely biological status is complicated by the concomitants of social status, and the results of studies of such people are difficult to interpret.

Cold adaptation

Man in the arctic provides another example of adaptations. In the **arctic**, however, people build houses, wear clothes, and light fires. These cultural traits constitute the predominant adaptations, and they are available for anyone to borrow. Thus, the Eskimos have designed fine arctic clothing, and European and American explorers have copied their **parkas** and **mukluks**. Furthermore, Eskimos have developed behavioural patterns to meet crises. William Laughlin, F. A. Milan, and others are contributing much to our knowledge of Eskimo adaptations. If one Eskimo falls into the water, a companion will immediately share half his dry clothing—enough to get both men home, cold but alive.

Despite cultural adaptations there are times when biological differences count. Baker gives an example of the **Yahgan** at the cold, southern tip of South America: we should not envision one

---

Peruvian Andes 秘鲁安第斯山脉

thorax 胸膛

modality 形态

Appalachian Mountain 阿帕拉契亚山脉

arctic 北极

parka 派克大衣
mukluk 高筒软靴

Yahgan 雅甘人

native dying of exposure in a snow-storm while a better-adapted companion survives; instead, cultural modes ordinarily modify the biological conditions; the family of the ill-adapted individual dies of starvation **huddled** at their campfire while the well-adapted counterparts comfortably collect shell-fish in the frigid water. To study cold-adaptation in man one must take account of indoor as well as outdoor temperatures, and also of activities, clothing, and shelter.

huddle 挤成一团

For life, man must maintain a core temperature close to 37°C. In the cold he does this by reducing circulation to the extremities. But the vessels of the extremities periodically dilate; this cold-induced "cycling" is a widespread phenomenon among mammals and must be adaptive in some way although it costs loss of stored heat. Body heat is generated by **metabolizing** food, burning it up as fuel. Shivering is an involuntary activity that increases the production of heat. All peoples of all places respond to cold in much the same ways. However, some people from cold climates (notably the Central Australian **aborigines**) have been reported to meet cold sleeping conditions by having the **extremities** cool off more relative to the trunk, and also by lowering core temperatures; but the subjects of these studies chewed tobacco and the leaves of Duboisia which contains an **alkaloid** poison. This cultural practice rather than genetic constitution may account for the difference in response. The short-run adaptations differ somewhat in those **inured** to the cold and in those new to it, but it is not definitely known how much genetic capacity for **acclimatization**, if any, differs among peoples.

metabolize 使新陈代谢

aborigine 土著居民
extremity 手足；四肢

alkaloid 生物碱

inured 习惯的
acclimatization 适应环境

In other species of animals, arctic forms tend to differ in predictable ways from those found in more southerly areas. One of the differences, fur, has no counterpart in man. The Eskimos, for instance, are relatively devoid of body hair. Arctic forms have small body-surface area relative to body mass. Some heat is lost in breathing, but most heat loss is through the skin; therefore the surface area of the skin (and hence the size of the individual, which largely determines surface area) relates to **dissipation** of heat. Body mass consists of metabolizing tissues (which produce heat) and fat (much of it just beneath the skin where it may help to **insulate**);

dissipation 消散

insulate 使隔热

hence increases in weight cause increased heat production and retention. Newman applies to man the two rules which express these relations between body size and form with temperature. Bergmann's rule states that, in bodies of the same shape, the larger one has relatively smaller surface area; cold-adapted animals therefore tend to be large. Allen's rule states that short extremities further increase the ratio of mass to surface area and that cold-adapted forms have relatively short limbs. In man, general body size as measured by weight or stature is, on the average, positively correlated with climate—especially the temperature in the coldest month. In continuous populations of large land areas of the Northern **Hemisphere**, including China, Europe, and the **contiguous** states of the United States, there is a **gradient** from larger average size in the north to smaller in the south. Nevertheless, these dimensions vary considerably in any one place.

hemisphere 半球

contiguous 邻近的

gradient 梯度；变化率

Other details of **morphology** may also relate to heat balance. Nose form seems to be adapted to the degree of need to moisten the air one inhales. Noses are narrower in colder zones. Although correlations of nasal dimensions with degree of **prognathism** and shape of the dental arch complicate interpretation, the average ratio of the width to the length of the nose of populations throughout the world is highly correlated with climate—especially with vapor pressure, the amount of moisture in a given amount of air. Of the various **Mongoloid** peoples, Eskimos have the narrowest noses. But it is unwise to assume that every morphological feature found in Eskimos is directly a protection against cold. For instance, the large, broad Mongoloid face of the Eskimo is more exposed to cold than the smaller face of the European, but frostbite of the face is rarely serious in both people.

morphology 形态学

prognathism 凸颚

Mongoloid 蒙古人种的

High altitudes are also cold, and altitude studies must deal with the influence of both altitude and temperature. Some individuals adapted to altitude and cold maintain warmer hands and feet than non-adapted controls. This may serve to maintain more oxygen in these tissues as well as meet the challenge of low temperature.

Heat Adaptation

The regulation of human responses to excessive heat involves at least two distinct types of environments—dry heat and humid heat. In a hot place when a person works hard, the temperature is extreme, the humidity is high, or the sunlight is excessive, it puts a **strain** on the temperature-regulation system of the body. After about a week of acclimatization to repeated heat stress a subject will improve his tolerance for these conditions through increased sweating and decreased **cardiovascular** strain.

Most species of **primates** live in tropical forest environments. In the view of many, man's ancestors at one stage also lived in a hot, humid zone with little movement of air and with little direct sunlight. Under those circumstances the heat is well tolerated during rest but hard work produces heat stress.

In drier and more open country at low latitudes, where it is possible that, at a later stage, man's **progenitors** evolved their upright posture and a hunting-gathering economy, sweat evaporates more readily but sunlight on man and on the objects about him add a severe radiant heat load to the problems of heat adaptation. Sweating remains important. The **upright** posture reduces the surface area exposed to direct sunlight compared to that of a **quadruped**. Whether hair, at least long, straight hair could be an added protection against heat is problematical. In any case nakedness, far from being an advantage, as some anthropologists have mistakenly claimed, would have prevented man from adapting to life under desert-like conditions until he achieved ready access to water through use of vessels or learned to wear loose clothing of some sort. Man cannot drink very much water at one time but can sweat more per hour than any other mammal so far tested. Before man learned how to carry water with him, human occupation of open plains and **savanna** therefore required behaviour that would make it easy to reach drinking water frequently.

Although man is unique in his heat-adaptive mechanisms, there is little **innate** difference between human groups in their ability to respond to heat stress. Short-term acclimatization aside, there is little evidence of population differences. Since heat absorption and dissipation are surface phenomena, the search for possible population differences is logically concentrated on the area of the

strain 压力

cardiovascular 心血管的

primate 灵长目动物

progenitor 祖先

upright 直立的
quadruped 四足动物

savanna 热带草原

innate 先天的；天生的

skin and the nature of its structures: **pigment granules**, hair, and sweat glands. Groups inhabiting the tropics are, as already noted, generally composed of small individuals. This increases the surface area relative to mass so that heat produced by activity can be more readily dissipated. Although even moderate activity in a hot environment normally results in some heat storage, excess heat must be dissipated sooner or later and this is more significant than the somewhat greater capacity for heat storage of larger individuals. In hot deserts the people are generally **lean**, another way of increasing the relative surface area and facilitating heat dissipation.

Pigment is not a simple question. Inhabitants of equatorial zones are dark. This is true of **Melanesia**, Australia, South India, and Africa, although in other respects the peoples of these areas are very different. Common adaptive modification rather than close common origins therefore accounts for the similarity in skin colour. Numerous theories have been advanced to explain why dark skin colour is adaptive in hot climates, and there is still no general agreement. Although light skin reflects more radiant heat, dark skin must protect the body better. Among other things dark skin inhibits sunburn, and sunburn interferes with the sweating response. Dark skin is also less susceptible to skin cancer, and it prevents the synthesis of too much vitamin D. In zones with much sun in summer, and little in the winter, the ability to **tan** in summer would therefore be an advantage. Marjorie Lee and I subjected individuals of various groups to measured amounts of **ultraviolet** light and we measured changes in the amount of light of different wavelengths reflected from the skin. We found that the capability to tan varies considerably between individuals—even those with similar initial pigmentation.

The chief pigment of skin is **melanin**, and control of its production is evidently **polygenic** but based on few **alleles** at few loci. Livingstone shows by computer simulation that on these assumptions one can easily account for the sort of skin colour distributions one encounters in going from north to south in Europe, the Near East, and Africa, if there is a small differential advantage of presence of dark colour in tropical Africa and vice versa in

---

pigment granule 色素粒

lean 瘦小的

Melanesia 美拉尼西亚（西南太平洋群岛）

tan 晒黑

ultraviolet 紫外线的

melanin 黑色素
polygenic 多基因的
allele 等位基因

Europe. His calculations include a variety of assumptions, including migrations between populations. They do not explain its basis, but they do show that adaptative natural selection for skin colour reasonably accounts for the known skin colour distribution.

The role of human differences in hair with respect to heat tolerance is hard to calculate. Sheep with thick wool can thereby stand very heavy exposure to direct sunlight. Perhaps the retention of head hair in human beings is related to the crown of the head being the most exposed part in the noonday sun, but the influence of hair of different colour and form remains to be established experimentally. Essentially nothing is known concerning when man's progenitors began to have such bald bodies or whether this **antedate**d the invention of cloaks and hats.

antedate 先于；早于

(2, 433 words)

❶ Recall

Answer the following questions with the information from the passage.

1. What is adaptation?
2. What is the central theme of the Darwinian theory of evolution?
3. How many levels does adaptation occur at?
4. What is the usual response when individuals climb from sea level to an elevation of 4,000 meters or more?
5. What are the three chief modalities of adaptation that mountain dwellers show?
6. How can a man maintain a core temperature close to 37°C in the cold?

❷ Interpret

Answer the following questions by analysing the passage.

7. At the beginning of Paragraph 9, the author says that arctic forms tend to differ in predictable ways from those found in more southerly areas. But at the end of Paragraph 10, the author states, "But it is unwise to assume that every morphological feature found in Eskimos is directly a protection against cold." Do you think that the author contradicts himself?

8. In Paragraph 12, the author mentions, "The regulation of human responses to excessive heat involves at least two distinct types of environments—dry heat and humid heat." How did our ancestors respond to dry heat and humid heat respectively?

Evaluate & Connect

Answer the following question by relating the passage to your own experience.

9. In Text A, the author focuses on human adaptation to altitude, cold, and heat. Based on Text A and your own knowledge, discuss human adaptation to other circumstances with specific examples.

 # Text B

Background Information

This text is adapted from the article "Tracing the Origins of Humans" published by *Science News* on September 25, 2021, which is an award-winning weekly news magazine covering important and emerging research in all fields of science. The article belongs to a series that shares some of the biggest advances in science over the last century to celebrate the magazine's 100th anniversary. It is authored by the Smithsonian's Erin Wayman, who is a science and human evolution blogger for Hominid Hunting. She has obtained her Master's degree in biological anthropology and science writing, and has published many articles in *Science News*. The present text probes into the origins of humans through the discovery of a fossil toddler, the Taung Child, in South Africa.

Tracing the Origins of Humans

Erin Wayman

In *The Descent of Man*, published in 1871, Charles Darwin hypothesized that our ancestors came from Africa. He pointed out that among all animals, the African apes—gorillas and chimpanzees—were the most similar to humans. But he had little fossil evidence. The few known human fossils had been found in Europe, and those that **trickled** in over the next 50 years came from Europe and from Asia.

Had Darwin picked the wrong continent?

Finally, in 1924, a **fortuitous** find supported Darwin's speculation. Among the **debris** at a limestone **quarry** in South Africa, miners recovered the fossilized skull of a **toddler**. Based on the child's blend of humanlike and apelike features, an anatomist determined that the fossil was what was then popularly known as a "missing link." It was the most apelike fossil yet found of a **hominid**—that is, a member of the family **Hominidae**, which includes modern humans and all our close, extinct relatives.

trickle 慢慢移动

fortuitous 偶然发生的
debris 残骸；碎片
quarry 采石场
toddler 学步的儿童
hominid 原始人类
Hominidae 人科

That fossil wasn't enough to confirm Africa as our homeland. Since that discovery, **paleoanthropologists** have amassed many thousands of fossils, and the evidence over and over again has pointed to Africa as our place of origin. Genetic studies reinforce that story. African apes are indeed our closest living relatives, with chimpanzees more closely related to us than to gorillas. In fact, many scientists now include great apes in the hominid family, using the narrower term "**hominin**" to refer to humans and our extinct cousins.

In a field with a reputation for bitter feuds and rivalries, the notion of humankind's African origins unifies human evolution researchers. "I think everybody agrees and understands that Africa was very **pivotal** in the evolution of our species," says Charles Musiba, a paleoanthropologist at the University of Colorado Denver.

Paleoanthropologists have sketched a rough timeline of how that evolution played out. Sometime between 9 million and 6 million years ago, the first hominins evolved. Walking upright on two legs distinguished our ancestors from other apes; our ancestors also had smaller **canine** teeth, perhaps a sign of less **aggression** and a change in social interactions. Between about 3.5 million and 3 million years ago, humankind's forerunners **ventured** beyond wooded areas. Africa was growing drier, and grasslands spread across the continent. Hominins were also **crafting** stone tools by this time. The human genus, *Homo*, arrived between 2.5 million and 2 million years ago, maybe earlier, with larger brains than their predecessors. By at least 2 million years ago, *Homo* members started traveling from Africa to Eurasia. By about 300,000 years ago, ***Homo sapiens***, our species, emerged.

But human evolution was not a gradual, linear process, as it appeared to be in the 1940s and '50s. It did not consist of a nearly unbroken chain, one hominin evolving into the next through time. Fossil discoveries in the '60s and '70s revealed a **bushier** family tree, with many dead-end branches. By some counts, more than 20 hominin species have been identified in the fossil record. Experts disagree on how to classify all of these forms—"Fossil species are mental constructs," a paleoanthropologist once told *Science News*—but clearly, hominins were diverse, with some species **overlapping** in both time and place.

Even our species wasn't always alone. Just 50,000 years ago, the diminutive, 1-meter-tall *Homo floresiensis*, nicknamed the **hobbit**, lived on the Indonesian island of Flores. And 300,000 years ago, *Homo naledi* was a neighbour in South Africa.

Finding such "primitive" species—both had relatively small brains—living at the same time as H. sapiens was a big surprise, says Bernard Wood, a paleoanthropologist at George Washington University in Washington, D.C. Those discoveries, made within the last two decades, were reminders of how much is left to learn.

It's premature to pen a comprehensive explanation of human evolution with so much ground—in Africa and elsewhere—to explore, Wood says. Our origin story is still a work in progress.

Eyes on Africa

Raymond Dart had a wedding to host.

It was a November afternoon in 1924, and the Australian-born anatomist was partially dressed in formal wear when he was distracted by fossils. Rocks containing the finds had just been brought to his home in Johannesburg, South Africa, from a mine near the town of **Taung**.

Imprinted on a knobby rock about as big as an orange were the folds, furrows and even blood vessels of a brain. It fit perfectly inside another rock that had a bit of jaw **peeking** out.

The **groom** pressed Dart to get back on track. "My god, Ray," he said. "You've got to finish dressing immediately—or I'll have to find another best man."

As soon as the **festivities** ended, Dart, 31 years old at the time, started removing the jaw from its limestone casing, chipping away with knitting needles. A few weeks later, he had liberated not just a jaw but a partial skull preserving the face of a child.

On February 7, 1925, in the journal *Nature*, Dart introduced the Taung Child to the world. He described the fossil as an ape like no other, one with some distinctly humanlike features, including a relatively flat face and fairly small canine teeth. The **foramen magnum**, the hole through which the spinal cord exits the head, was positioned directly under the skull, implying the child had an erect posture and walked on two legs.

Dart concluded that the Taung Child belonged to "an extinct race of apes *intermediate between living **anthropoids** and man.*" His italicized text emphasized his judgment: The fossil was a so-called missing link between other **primates** and humans. He named it ***Australopithecus africanus***, or southern ape of Africa.

The Taung Child was the second hominin fossil discovered in Africa, and much more primitive than the first. Dart argued that the find vindicated Darwin's belief that humans arose on that continent. "There seems to be little doubt," *Science News Letter*, the predecessor of *Science News*, reported, "that there has been discovered on the reputed 'dark' continent a most important step in the evolutionary history of man."

But Dart's claims were mostly met with scepticism. It would take more than two decades of new fossil finds and advances in geologic dating for Dart to be vindicated—and for Africa to become the **epicentre** of palaeoanthropology.

Against the establishment

Unlike Darwin, many evolutionists of the late 19th and early 20th centuries had theorized that the human family tree was rooted in Asia. Some argued that Asia's **gibbons** were our closest living relatives. Others reasoned that **tectonic** activity and climate change in Central Asia sparked human evolution. One naturalist even proposed that human origins traced back to a lost continent that had sunk in the Indian Ocean, forcing our ancestors to relocate to Southeast Asia.

And that's where the best contender for an early human ancestor had been found. In the 1890s, a crew led by Dutch physician-turned-anthropologist Eugène Dubois had uncovered a **skullcap** and thigh bone on the Indonesian island of **Java**. The thick skullcap had heavy brow ridges, but Dubois estimated it once held a brain that was about twice as big as an ape's and approaching the size of a human's. The thigh bone indicated that this Java Man, later named **Homo erectus**, walked upright.

---

anthropoid 类人猿

primate 灵长目动物（包括人、猴子等）

Australopithecus africanus 非洲南方古猿

epicentre 中心

gibbon 长臂猿

tectonic 地壳构造上的

skullcap 头盖骨

Java 爪哇岛（位于印尼）

Homo erectus 直立人

Europe had its own **tantalizing** fossils. **Neandertals** had been known since the mid-19th century, but by the early 20th century, they were generally thought to be cousins that lived too recently to shed much light on our early evolution. A more relevant discovery seemed to come in 1912, when an amateur **archaeologist** had recovered humanlike bones from near **Piltdown**, England; the site also contained fossils of extinct creatures, suggesting Piltdown Man was of great antiquity. Skull bones hinted he had a human-sized brain, but his primitive jaw had a large, apelike canine tooth.

Some experts questioned whether the skull and jaw belonged together. But British scientists embraced the discovery—and not just because it implied England had a role in human origins. Piltdown Man's features fit with the British establishment's view of human evolution, in which a big brain was the first trait to distinguish human ancestors from other apes.

So when Dart announced that he had found a small-brained **bipedal** ape with humanlike teeth in the southern **tip** of Africa, scientists were primed to be sceptical, says Paige Madison, a historian of science at the Natural History Museum of Denmark in Copenhagen. Scientists were also sceptical of Dart. While a student in London, he had earned a reputation as a "scientific heretic, given to sweeping claims," according to a paper coauthored by a colleague.

But initial criticism focused mostly on practical concerns, says Madison, who has studied the sceptics' reactions. "I found what they were actually saying on paper to be quite reasonable."

A big problem: Dart's fossil was of a 3- or 4-year-old child. Critics pointed out that a young ape tends to resemble humans in some ways, but the similarities disappear as the ape matures. Critics also complained that Dart hadn't done proper comparative analyses with young **chimps** and **gorillas**, and he refused to send the fossil to England where such analyses could be done. This refusal **irked** the British old guard. "It was **unpalatable** to the scientists in England that the young colonial **upstart** had presumed to describe the skull himself," one of Dart's contemporaries later wrote, "instead of submitting it to his elders and betters."

It's hard not to wonder how the era's colonialist and racist attitudes shaped perceptions. The Taung Child came to light at a time when **eugenics** was still considered legitimate science, and much of anthropology was devoted to categorizing people into races and arranging them into hierarchies. On the one hand, Western researchers tended to maintain the perverse notion that Africans are more primitive than other people, even less evolved. On the other, they wanted to believe Europe or Asia is where humans originated.

How these views influenced reactions to the Taung Child is not clear-cut. Many sceptics didn't cite the fossil's location as a problem, and some acknowledged humans could have evolved in Africa. But deep-seated biases may have made it easier for some researchers to reject the Taung Child and accept Piltdown Man, even though fossil evidence for that claim was also scant, says **Sheela Athreya**, a paleoanthropologist at Texas A&M University in College Station.

Newspapers worldwide followed the Taung Child controversy. And while fans sent Dart poems and short stories casting the child as a national hero, he also received letters from disapproving creationists.

Amid it all, Dart had convinced at least one well-known scientist. **Robert Broom**, a Scottish-born physician living in South Africa and an authority on **reptile** evolution, recognized that fossils of fully grown *A. africanus* individuals would be needed to confirm that the Taung Child's humanlike qualities were retained in adulthood.

Broom began to find just that evidence in 1936 in caves not far from **Johannesburg**. Often taking the heavy-handed approach of detonating dynamite to free specimens, he amassed a collection of fossils representing both the young and the old. Limb, spine and hip bones confirmed South Africa was once home to a bipedal ape, and skull bones verified Dart's inferences about *A. africanus*' humanlike teeth.

Even the staunchest Dart doubters couldn't overlook this evidence. British anatomist **Arthur Keith**, who had once called Dart's assertions "preposterous," conceded. "I am now convinced," he wrote in a one-paragraph letter to *Nature* in 1947, "that Prof. Dart was right and that I was wrong; the **Australopithecine** are in or near the line which culminated in the human form."

A few years later, in 1953, researchers exposed Piltdown Man to be a hoax—someone had planted a modern human skull alongside an **orangutan** jaw with its teeth **filed down**. Many experts outside of England had never been convinced by the find in the first place. "It was not a complete surprise when he was proved to be a fake," *Science News Letter* reported.

Still, Africa's role in human evolution was not **cemented**. From the time of the Taung Child's unearthing through World War II, discoveries of hominin fossils continued in Indonesia and at a cave site near Beijing called Zhoukoudian. These fossils kept the focus on Asia.

On the origin of our species

Even after it became clear that hominins originated in Africa, it was still uncertain where our species, *Homo sapiens*, began. By the 1980s, paleoanthropologists had largely settled into two camps. One side claimed that, like the earliest hominins, modern humans came from someplace in Africa. The other side championed a more **diffuse** start across Africa, Asia and Europe.

That same decade saw researchers increasingly relying on genetics to study human origins. Initially, scientists looked to modern people's DNA to make inferences about ancient populations. But by the late 1990s, geneticists **pulled off** a feat straight out of science fiction: decoding DNA preserved in hominin fossils.

For paleoanthropologists, studying ancient DNA has been like astronomers getting a new telescope that sees into deep space with a new wavelength of light. It's revealing things no one even thought to look for, says paleoanthropologist **John Hawks** of the University of Wisconsin–Madison. "That is the most powerful thing that genetics has handed us."

And it's revealed a truly **tangled** tale.

(2, 220 Words)

Unit 7 Life Science

❶ Recall

Answer the following questions with the information from the passage.

1. According to Charles Darwin, what animals were the most similar to humans?
2. What's the term many scientists now use to refer to humans and our extinct cousins?
3. When did our species Homo sapiens emerge?
4. How did Dart describe the Taung Child in the journal *Nature* in 1925?
5. According to Dart, what did the find of the Taung Child vindicate?
6. What was the British establishment's view of human evolution?

❷ Interpret

Answer the following questions by analysing the passage.

7. In the text, the author states, "It's hard not to wonder how the era's colonialist and racist attitudes shaped perceptions. " What were the era's colonialist and racist attitudes?
8. In the text, the author mentions, "Still, Africa's role in human evolution was not cemented." Please explain the reasons according to the text.

❸ Evaluate & Connect

Answer the following question by relating the passage to your own experience.

9. In Text B, the author says, "For paleoanthropologists, studying ancient DNA has been like astronomers getting a new telescope that sees into deep space with a new wavelength of light." Please elaborate the benefits of decoding ancient DNA in tracing the origins of humans.

Earth and Space Science

Synopsis

  我们赖以生存的地球是如何形成与演化的？地球所在的太阳系是怎么样的？基于对"地球与空间科学"主题的探索，我们将一起了解地球与宇宙空间的奥秘。随着科技的发展，人类的脚步已踏入太空，地球和宇宙也在人类一步步的探索中被揭开了神秘的面纱。本单元 Text A 通过"太阳系的形成"和"陨石说地球"介绍太阳系和地球的形成；Text B 重点讲述了科学家对地球年龄的探究。

Warm-up

Below are the eight planets of the Solar System. Do you know their names? Write down the name of each planet and share what you know about them.

①:　　　　②:　　　　③:　　　　④:

⑤:　　　　⑥:　　　　⑦:　　　　⑧:

Text A

Background information

This article is extracted from *Origin and Evolution of Earth: Research Questions for a Changing Planet* published by National Academies Press in 2008. The subject of this report was approved by the Governing Board of the National Research Council, whose members are drawn from the councils of the National Academy of Sciences, the National Academy of Engineering, and the Institute of Medicine. This book captures, in a series of questions, the essential scientific challenges that constitute the frontier of Earth science at the start of the 21st century. Questions about the origin and nature of Earth and the life on it have long preoccupied human thought and scientific endeavour. Deciphering the planet's history and processes could improve the ability to predict catastrophes like earthquakes and volcanic eruptions, manage Earth's resources, and anticipate changes in climate and geologic processes.

How Did Earth and Other Planets Form?

National Research Council

The modern study of Earth is ultimately rooted in humankind's desire to understand its origins. Although it was once assumed that intelligent life was unique to Earth, we have now gained an appreciation that even though it may not be unique, the existence of advanced life on planets may well be uncommon. None of the other planets of the Solar System are presently suitable for the complex life forms that exist on Earth, and we have yet to identify other stars that have planets much like Earth. Although the odds are good that there is other life in our galaxy, this **inference** has not been confirmed.

| inference 推论 |

Considering the apparent rarity of Earth-like life, it is natural to want to understand what went into making Earth suitable for life and how life arose. Pursuing these questions leads us to fundamental issues about how stars and planets form and evolve and to questions about how the modern Earth works, from the innermost core to

the atmosphere, oceans, and land surface. This article presents the question related specifically to origins—one regarding the origin of Earth and other planets. These questions are separated by two questions that deals: **1) How did the solar system planets form? 2) What do meteorites say about the origin of earth,** which mainly talks about Earth's earliest history: the 500 million to 700 million years between the time of the origin of the Solar System and the oldest significant rock record preserved on Earth. During this early, still poorly understood, stage of Earth's development, tremendous changes must have taken place, accompanied by myriad **catastrophic** events, all leading ultimately to a setting in which life could develop and eventually thrive.

meteorite 陨石

catastrophic 灾难性的

One of the most challenging and relevant questions about Earth's formation is why our planet is the only one in the Solar System with abundant liquid water at its surface and abundant carbon in forms that can be used to make organic matter. This question is part of a broader set: why the inner planets are rocky and the outer planets are gaseous; how the growth and orbital evolution of the outer planets influenced the inner Solar System; why all of the largest planets are so different from one another; and how typical our Solar System is within the **Milky Way galaxy**. Although these questions are longstanding, the answers are only now emerging from new insights provided by astronomy, **isotopic chemistry**, Solar System exploration, and advanced computing. And although we know in general how to make a planet like Earth—starting with some stardust and allowing gravity, radiation, and **thermodynamics** to do their parts—our answers often serve only to refine our questions. For example, the details of Earth's chemical composition—such as how much of the heat-producing elements **uranium, thorium,** and **potassium** it contains; how much oxygen and carbon it contains; and how it came to have its particular **allotment** of noble gases and other minor constituents—turn out to be critical to models of Earth's geological processes and, ultimately, to understanding why Earth has remained suitable for life over most of its history.

Milky Way galaxy 银河系

isotopic chemistry 同位素化学

thermodynamics 热力学

uranium 铀
thorium 钍
potassium 钾
allotment 分配

1. How did the solar system planets form?

The Solar System is composed of radically different types of planets. The outer planets (Jupiter, Saturn, Uranus, and Neptune) are distinguished from the inner planets by their large size and low **density**. The outer planets are the primary products of the planet formation process and comprise almost all of the mass held in the planetary system. They are also the types of planets that are most easily recognized orbiting other stars. The inner planets (Mercury, Venus, Earth, and Mars) are composed mostly of rock and metal, with only minor amounts of gaseous material. There are "standard models" for the formation of both types of planets, but they have serious deficiencies and large uncertainties.

According to the standard model for outer-planet formation, the formation of giant planets starts with **condensation** and **coalescence** of rocky and icy material to form objects several times as massive as Earth. These solid bodies then attract and accumulate gas from the **circumstellar** disk. The two largest outer planets, Jupiter and Saturn, seem to fit this model reasonably well, as they consist primarily of **hydrogen** and **helium** in roughly solar proportions, but they also include several Earth masses of heavier elements in greater than solar proportions, probably residing in a dense central core. Uranus and Neptune, however, have much lower abundances of hydrogen and helium than Jupiter and Saturn and have densities and atmospheric compositions consistent with a significant component of outer Solar System ices.

An alternative to the standard model is that the rock and ice balls are not needed to induce the formation of gas-giant planets; they can form directly from the gas and dust in the disk, which can **collapse** under its own gravity like mini-versions of the Sun. In this model the excess abundances of heavy elements in Jupiter and Saturn would have been acquired later by capture of smaller rocky and icy bodies. This model, however, does not account well for the compositions of Uranus and Neptune, which do not have very much gas. Other important questions about the outer planets are when they formed and the extent to which they may have drifted inward or outward from the Sun during and after formation. Where the outer planets were and when is important for understanding how the inner planets formed.

density 密度

condensation 冷凝
coalescence 凝聚；聚合
circumstellar 环绕恒星的
hydrogen 氢
helium 氦

collapse 瓦解

The primary difference between the inner and outer planets (rock versus gas and ice) is thought to reflect the temperature gradient in the solar **nebula**. Temperatures were relatively high (1,000 K) near the developing Sun, dropping steadily with distance. Near the Sun, mainly **silicates** and metal would have condensed from the gas (so-called refractory materials), whereas beyond the **asteroid belt**, temperatures were low enough for ices (i.e., water, **methane**, **ammonia**) containing more **volatile** elements to have condensed, as well as solid silicates. It was once thought that as the nebula cooled, solids formed in a simple unidirectional process of condensation. We now know that solids typically were re-melted, re-evaporated, and re-condensed repeatedly as materials were circulated through different temperature regimes and variously affected by nebular shock waves and collisions between solid objects. Important details of the temperatures of the solar nebula, however, are still uncertain, including such significant issues as peak temperatures, how long they were maintained, and how temperature varied with distance from the Sun and from the midplane of the disk. Defining these conditions is an important part of understanding how the chemical compositions of the planets and meteorites came to be.

The standard model for the formation of the inner planets is somewhat more complicated than the model for outer-planet formation and is based largely on theory and anchored in information from meteorites and observations of disks around other stars. The model strives to explain how a dispersed **molecular** cloud with a small amount of dust could evolve into solid planets with virtually no intervening gas and how the original mix of chemical elements in the molecular cloud was modified during that evolution. Significant unknowns are how long the process took, how solid materials were able to **coagulate** into progressively larger bodies, and how and when the residual gas was dissipated. The time for centimetre-sized solid objects to form at Earth's distance from the Sun, according to the standard model, might have been as short as 10,000 years. These small solid objects were highly mobile, pulled Sun-ward large distances by the Sun's gravity as a result of drag from the still-present H-He gas. Submeter-sized objects were also strongly affected by turbulence in the gas.

---

nebula 星云

silicates 硅酸盐

asteroid belt 小行星带

methane 甲烷

ammonia 氨

volatile 挥发性的

molecular 分子状态

coagulate 凝固

A particular **deficiency** of the standard model is its inability to describe the formation of kilometre-sized bodies from smaller fragments. The current best guess is that the dust grains aggregated slowly at first, and growth accelerated along with object size as small objects were embedded into larger ones. The **aggregation** behaviour of objects greater than a kilometre in size is better understood: they are less affected by the presence of gas than are smaller pieces, and their subsequent evolution is governed by mutual gravitational attractions. Growth of still larger bodies, or **planetesimals**, from these kilometre-sized pieces should have been more rapid, especially at first. Gravitational interactions gave the largest planetesimals nearly circular and **coplanar** orbits—the most favourable conditions for sweeping up smaller objects. This led to runaway growth and formation of Moon-to-Mars-sized planetary **embryos**. Growth would have slowed when the supply of small planetesimals was depleted and the embryos evolved onto inclined, **elliptical** orbits. Dynamical simulations based on statistical methods and specialized computer codes are finding that a number of closely spaced planetary embryos are likely to have formed about 100,000 years after planetesimals appeared in large numbers.

The later stages of planet formation took much longer, involved progressively fewer objects, and hence are less predictable (Figure 1). The main phase of **terrestrial** planet formation probably took a few tens of millions of years. The final stages were marked by the occasional collision and merger of planetary embryos, which continued until the orbits of the resulting planets separated sufficiently to be protected from additional major collisions.

Although there are four terrestrial planets, models suggest that the number could easily have been three or five, and they would have been at different distances from the Sun. Tidal interactions with nebular gas may have caused early-formed inner planets to migrate inward substantially while they were forming, and several planets may have been lost into the Sun before the gas dispersed. The fact that there are no rocky planets beyond Mars is likely a consequence of the presence of the giant planets, particularly Jupiter. The large mass and strong gravitational pull of Jupiter probably prevented the

deficiency 不足

aggregation 聚集

planetesimals 小行星体

coplanar 共面的

embryo 胚胎

elliptical 椭圆的

terrestrial 类地行星的

formation of additional rocky planets in the region now occupied by the asteroid belt by disrupting the orbits of bodies in that region before they could form a large planet. Jupiter and Saturn also sent objects from the asteroid belt either out of the Solar System or spiralling into the inner-planet region where they became parts of the planets forming there or fell into the Sun. The asteroids represent the 0.01% of material that survived this process.

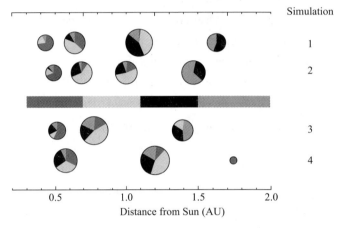

Figure 1 Results of four representative numerical simulations of the final stage of accretion of the terrestrial planets. The segments in each pie show the fraction of material originating from the four regions of the solar nebula shown by the shades of gray, and the size of the pie is proportional to the volume of each planet In each simulation the largest planet has a size similar to the Earth, but there can be either two or three other planets, and the sizes vary. The planets typically receive materialfrom all four zones, with preference for the zones closest to their final orbit location.

2. What do meteorites say about of the earth?

Earth has undergone so much geological change that we find little evidence in rocks about its origin or even its early development. Many meteorites, on the other hand, were not affected by the high-temperature processing that occurs in planetary interiors. They are fragments of, or soil samples from, miniplanets that formed in what is now the asteroid belt just as the Solar System was starting out. Thus, they preserve significant clues about the state of the Solar System when the planets were forming. For this reason, studies of meteorites play a major role in helping us understand Earth's origin.

One gift of meteorites is to reveal the age of the Solar System. Precise radiometric dating of high-temperature inclusions within meteorites shows that the first solid objects in our home system formed 4,567 million years ago. We also know that shortly thereafter planetesimals of rock and metal formed and developed iron-rich cores and rocky crusts. Some meteorites are chemically like the Sun (for elements other than H, He, Li, C, N, O, and noble gases), and some of these same meteorites contain tiny mineral grains of dust that survived from earlier generations of stars. Other meteorites are parts of small planetary bodies that experienced early volcanism and that were later broken up by collisions. Beyond these clues, meteorites fall short of providing all the information needed to understand Earth, partly because most of them formed far from the Sun (the main asteroid belt is between Mars and Jupiter), and the relationship between meteorites and planets is not fully understood. The systematic collection of well-preserved samples from Antarctica has greatly expanded the number of meteorites available for study and has yielded rarities such as meteorites from Mars and the Moon.

Figure 2 The Allende meteorite, a carbonaceous chondrite, is a mixture of CAIs (calcium-, aluminum-rich inclusions; larger irregularly shaped light-colored objects) and chondrules (round light-colored objects) in a dark-colored matrix of minerals and compounds. The CAIs and chondrules are a high-temperature component that formed and were in some cases reprocessed at temperatures above 1,000 ℃.

Beyond what they tell us about Earth, meteorites provide a benchmark for understanding the composition of the Sun and even the Universe as a whole. Most of the visible mass of the Universe, and almost all stars, is composed primarily of hydrogen and helium made during the Big Bang. The rest of the elements—the "heavier" ones with more **protons** and **neutrons** in their nuclei—were produced by **nucleon-synthesis**, or **thermonuclear** reactions within stars.

protons 质子
neutrons 中子
nucleon-synthesis 核合成
thermonuclear 高热原子核反应的

Most nucleon-synthesis happens in big stars. These massive stars last only about 10 million to 20 million years before they explode as **supernovae**. The new elements they make, before and during the explosion, are thrown back into space where they are later recycled into new stars. In the approximately 10 billion years between the origin of the Universe and the origin of the Solar System, hundreds of generations of massive stars have exploded, and over this long period about 1% (by weight) of the original H and He has been converted to heavier elements. Meteorites give us the most detailed information about the abundances of these heavier elements.

Meteorites tell us still more about the formation of the Solar System out of the nebular disk. The abundance of heavy elements in the Sun is known moderately well from **spectroscopic** data. The planets, however, formed from the nebular disk, so it is important to know whether the disk had the same composition as the Sun, and whether it was **homogeneous** or varied significantly in composition, perhaps with **radial** distance from the proto-Sun. The standard model for the composition of the solar nebula is based on studies of a class of meteorites called **chondrites**. Chondrites, the commonest type of meteorites, are stony bodies formed from the accretion of dust and small grains that were present in the early Solar System. They are often used as reference points for chemicals present in the original solar nebula. The most primitive of these objects—those least altered by heat and pressure—are carbonaceous chondrites, whose chemical compositions match that of the Sun for most elements. The relative amounts of elements and their isotopes can be measured much more precisely on meteoritic materials than by solar **spectroscopy**, so chondritic meteorites play a special role in helping to understand both Earth and nucleosynthesis in our galaxy. Because chondritic elemental abundances look similar to those of the Sun, the disk likely had about the same composition as the Sun.

(2,413 words)

supernovae 超新星

spectroscopic 光谱仪的

homogeneous 同质的
radial 径向的

chondrites 球粒状陨石

spectroscopy 光谱学

Unit 8 Earth and Space Science

❶ Recall

Answer the following questions with the information from the passage.

1. What can separate the inner planets from the outer planets?
2. What is the difference between the inner and the outer planets?
3. What do meteorites say about the origin of Earth?
4. According to the standard model of outer-planet formation, how did Jupiter form?
5. Based on the standard model for the formation of the inner planets, how to explain the formation of kilometre-sized bodies from smaller fragments?

❷ Interpret

Answer the following questions by analysing the passage.

6. How many models for the formation of planets are mentioned in this article? What are they?
7. What kind of information can we learn from meteorites?
8. Why are there no rocky planets beyond Mars?

❸ Evaluate & Connect

Read the following information. Answer the questions by relating the passage to your own experience.

9. The English astronomer Edmond Halley (1656—1742) once proposed a method to estimate the origin of the Earth. He reasoned as follows: The rivers, as they flow, dissolve tiny quantities of salt from the land they flow through and deliver them to the ocean. The salt stays in the ocean, because only the watery portion of the sea evaporates under the action of the Sun. This water vapor falls as rain, which contains no salt to speak of, but as the rivers return the fallen water to the ocean, they deliver a bit more dissolved salt from the land. This happens over and over again. If we suppose that the ocean was fresh water to begin with, and if we measure how much salt is being added to it each year, then we can calculate how many years that salt must have been added to cause the ocean to be 3.3% salt as it is today. What do you think of this method? Is it reasonable or not? Why?

Text B

Background information

This article is extracted from *Beginnings: The story of origins, of mankind, life, the Earth, the Universe* written by Isaac Asimov in 1987. This book begins with the origins of human flight. In a series of logically connected chapters, it moves smoothly through the origins of human history, humankind, animals and plants, cells, and the earth, and endings on the origin of the universe. Isaac Asimov authored over 400 books in a career that lasted nearly 50 years and won numerous awards. As a leading science writer, historian, and futurist, he covered a variety of subjects ranging from mathematics to humour.

The Age of Earth

Isaac Asimov

The origin of Earth has been a subject of great interest among scientists for a long time. Actually, there was no sensible way of estimating the age of the Earth until the **uniformitarian** principle was established. Once it was accepted that slow changes were taking place over long periods of time, the system for estimating Earth's age was clear. One must calculate the rate at which a particular slow change was taking place, determine the total change that has taken place, and then divide the latter by the former.

The first attempt to do this came in 1715, when the English astronomer Edmond Halley (1656—1742) reasoned as follows: The rivers, as they flow, dissolve tiny quantities of salt from the land they flow through and deliver them to the ocean. The salt stays in the ocean, for only the watery portion of the sea **evaporates** under the action of the Sun. This water vapor falls as rain, which contains no salt to speak of, but as the rivers return the fallen water to the ocean, they deliver a bit more dissolved salt from the land. This happens over and over again. If we suppose that the ocean was fresh water to

uniformitarian 均变论的

evaporate 蒸发

begin with, and if we measure how much salt is being added to it each year, then we can calculate how many years that salt must have been added to cause the ocean to be 3.3% salt, as it is today.

In principle, this is a straightforward and very simple arithmetical operation, but there were many gaping holes in it. First, it might be that the ocean didn't start as fresh water but had salt in it to begin with. Second, it was quite impossible for Halley, in his time, to know the exact rate at which salt was being added to the ocean each year because many rivers outside Europe had never been chemically analysed and even the volume delivered could not be accurately known. One had to estimate, judging by the rivers one knew, and the estimate might easily be wildly wrong. Third, there was no way of knowing whether the rate of salt delivery to the ocean really remained constant year after year. Rivers might be more **turbulent** or more placid at certain periods of Earth's lifetime, and the present state might be nowhere near the average. Fourth, there were processes that could remove salt from the ocean. Storm winds send ocean spray, with its salt content, over the land. Shallow arms of the ocean can dry up completely, leaving their salt content behind (which is where salt mines come from). Taking this all into account, it would therefore be quite possible for Halley to end up with a figure that was dreadfully wrong.

His estimate was, in fact, that Earth's ocean might be as much as 1,000 million years old. This, actually, was quite a respectable estimate for the first time round. At the time, though, it made little impression. Ussher's decision still held sway at that time, and it was easy to maintain that Earth was created 6,000 years ago with an ocean containing today`s level of salt.

Another way of estimating the Earth's age depended upon **sedimentation** rates. The rivers, lakes, and oceans of the world laid down mud and **sludg**e—sediment—and such sediment, under the weight of further layers laid down about it, was compressed into sedimentary rock. Since the watery parts of the globe were rich in life, it frequently happened that living things, recently dead ones, or parts of them were trapped in the sediment under conditions that made for fossilization. Even land animals had to find water periodically and

turbulent 汹涌的

sedimentation 沉淀
sludge 沉淀物

might be trapped in waterholes, or killed there, and somehow end up in the sedimentary rock as fossils.

Fossil hunters could measure the thickness of the sedimentary rock in which they found fossils. If the rate of sedimentation could be determined, then from the thickness of the strata representing a particular geological period the duration of that period could be calculated. Once the periods were put in order, the total duration for all of them and the time **lapse** since the present could be determined.

lapse 时间的流逝

This was not a very accurate way of measuring the age of the fossils, for it was impossible to say whether the sedimentation rate was the same in one place as in another, or at one time as in another. Variations were so great (and sometimes not really known) that no calculated average could really be trusted. Still, estimates were advanced to the effect that the oldest fossils were perhaps 500 million years old, and that was not at all bad for dealing with something as uncertain as sedimentation. It was against this background of an Earth that was possibly 500 million years old or more that Darwin was able to **postulate** a scheme of biological evolution involving random variations, with natural selection serving to remove the randomness and to lend the process the illusion of purpose. This was bound to be a very slow process and it needed hundreds of millions of years of time.

postulate 假设

In the 1840s it was becoming more and more clear that energy could neither be created nor destroyed. The Universe, it seemed, had a fixed supply of energy, which could be converted from one form to another, but which remained unchanged in total amount. This is called the **law of conservation of energy** or **the first law of thermodynamics** and is, to this day, considered the most basic of all the laws of nature. It was formally stated by the German physicist Hermann L. F. von Helmholtz (1821—1894) in 1847.

law of conservation of energy
能量守恒定律

first law of thermodynamics
热力学第一定律

The Scottish physicist William Thomson, Lord Kelvin (1824—1907) took up the matter and by 1862 had calculated that 50 million years ago the Sun had extended out to Earth's orbit. In other words, if the Sun had started out filling Earth's orbit and had contracted to its present size it would have emitted energy at its present rate for only

50 million years. That meant that earth had to be no more than 50 million years old and could not have supported life until the Sun had contracted sufficiently to leave Earth comparatively cool. Life, then, would be far less than 50 million years old.

This horrified both geologists and biologists, who were absolutely certain that the Earth was far older than that. Kelvin's suggested age was, by his time, as ridiculously small to those who studied the slow changes in the Earth's crust and in evolutionary development as Ussher's suggested age was.

Yet how could one argue with the law of conservation of energy? All that the biologists and geologists could do was to insist that somewhere, somehow, there was another source of energy, one that was bigger and better than solar contraction, that would account for the Sun's energy over at least ten to twenty times the period that Kelvin allowed.

The solution both to the age of the Earth and to the energy source of the Sun arose out of a discovery by the French physicist Antoine Henri Becquerel (1852—1908).

In 1896 he accidentally discovered that the element **uranium** slowly but steadily gave off energetic radiations. The Polish-French physicist Marie Sklodowska Curie (1867—1934) discovered in 1898 that the element **thorium** also gave off energetic radiation, and she named the phenomenon **radioactivity**.

uranium 铀

thorium 钍
radioactivity 放射性

The uranium and thorium, in giving off this radiation, were producing energy. Pierre Curie (1859—1906), the husband of Marie, was the first, in 1901, to measure the energy production, and he was able to show that the total energy a given weight of uranium emitted was enormously higher than the energy given off by the same weight of burning coal. The radioactive energies are given off so slowly, however that only delicate measurements reveal its existence. The New Zealand-born British physicist Ernest Rutherford (1871—1937) suggested in 1904 that this new source of energy, in some form, must be the answer to the problem of the Sun's energy. It was so incredibly rich a source that it would allow the Sun to shine for billions of years without perceptible change. That would allow the Earth to be as old as geologists and biologists said it was.

He said this in a public lecture with the aged Kelvin himself in the audience. But what was the precise source of this energy of radioactivity? None was apparent at first. Did this mean, then, that the law of conservation of energy would have to be abandoned? It did not have to be. Rutherford allowed radioactive radiations to **smash** into intact atoms and the result made it plain that the atom was not just an ultra-tiny featureless ball as chemists had assumed it to be throughout the nineteenth century. By 1911, he showed that atoms consisted of a very tiny nucleus at the centre, a nucleus only 1/100,000 the **diameter** of the atom as a whole. Almost all the atomic mass is in that tiny nucleus. Around it, filling the rest of the atom, is a froth of light **electrons**. Ordinary energy obtained from chemical change, such as in the burning of fuel or in the explosion of **dynamite**, results from alterations in the arrangements of the light electrons. The much greater energies of radioactivity result from alterations in the much more massive particles within the tiny nucleus. In this way, nuclear energy was discovered.

smash 因猛烈地撞击而破碎

diameter 直径

electron 电子

dynamite 炸药

Clearly, then, the Sun must be powered by nuclear energy, though the exact details were not worked out for another twenty years. And as though that were not enough, the phenomenon of radioactivity served another purpose, too, that was in its way just as exciting.

Scientists quickly discovered that when a radioactive atom gave off energetic radiation, its nucleus rearranged itself so that the atom became different in nature. In 1904, the American physicist Bertram Borden Boltwood (1870—1927) pointed out that as uranium (or thorium) broke down it formed another kind of atom that also broke down, giving off radiations to form a third kind that broke down, and so on. Thus, one could speak of a radioactive series. Boltwood also pointed out that the final atom in both the uranium series and the thorium series was lead. The lead atom that was produced in the series was not radioactive and it changed no further. The net effect of this kind of radioactivity, then, was to change uranium or thorium into lead.

In that same year of 1904, Rutherford showed that a particular radioactive substance always acted so that half of any quantity always broke down in the same particular length of time. This length of time he called the **half-life**. Each different radioactive substance has a different half-life, in some cases a tiny fraction of a second; in others, thousands of millions of years; and in still others, anywhere in between. A given substance always has the same half-life, at least under earthly conditions. If the half-life of a particular radioactive substance is known, it is easy to calculate how much of it will be left after any given time.

Boltwood suggested in 1907 that if a rock contained uranium, some of it was bound to be very slowly transforming itself into lead. From the amount of lead that had accumulated in the rock in association with the uranium, you could calculate how long the rock had existed in solid form. (As long as the rock was solid, neither the uranium nor the lead could escape from it.)

Since the half-life of uranium is 4,500 million years and that of thorium 14,000 million years, then even if the Earth were many thousands of millions of years old, not all of the uranium or thorium would have had time to break down and you would still be able to calculate the age of the rock.

As it happens, uranium and thorium are present in a wide variety of Earth's rocks, so that almost any of them can be easily dated. To be sure, the uranium and thorium are present in small quantities, but the detection of radioactive substances is a very precise procedure and small quantities are all that are needed. Another element, **rubidium**, that is less common than potassium, has fully one-quarter of its atoms as rubidium-87, which is radioactive and has a half-life of 46,000 million years, breaking down into **strontium**-87, which is stable. Both **potassium** and rubidium can also be used to determine great ages with considerable accuracy.

To be sure, although the principle of age measurement by radioactive breakdown is quite simple and straightforward, the practice can be difficult. Rocks have to be sampled carefully, delicate radioactive measurements have to be made over and over, there has to be some way of determining whether any lead (or strontium, or argon) was present to begin with, having no relationship to radioactive breakdown, and so on. Nevertheless, methods were worked out and

---

half-life 半衰期

rubidium 铷

strontium 锶
potassium 钾

made practical, and the durations of the various geological periods, and the time before the present in which they existed, were calculated. In fact, rocks were discovered that were older than any that we have considered so far. The oldest rock so far found seems to be 3,800 million years old, give or take a hundred million years.

This represents a minimum age for the Earth, for the older a rock is the less likely it is to be found reasonably untouched during all its existence. Rocks may be eroded by the action of wind, water, or life; or they may be carried far down into the earth by plate movement and melted. It may be, then, that rocks older than 3,800 million years exist but are so rare that they have not been found, or perhaps, indeed, no rocks have survived for longer than that period.

In 2001 Australian researchers announced the discovery of a small grain of **zircon** (a mineral containing zirconium) that they dated to 4.4 billion years ago. Moreover, **meteorites**, which likely formed at about the same time as Earth, have been dated to about 4.5 billion years ago. These findings help pin down a likely age of about 4.55 billion years for Earth itself. Nevertheless, scientists have been able, from the changing proportions of rubidium and strontium in rocks, to reason out when the Earth first assumed something like its present size and structure. What seems most likely now is that the Earth formed 4,550 million years ago.

zircon 锆石
meteorites 陨星

Such a figure gives us a completely different perspective on geologic time. The first **chordates** appeared 550 million years ago, which would naturally seem like an event that had taken place in an unimaginably distant past. And yet, as a matter of fact, we now see that it happened rather recently. Moving 550 million years into the past take us only through the last eighth of Earth's history. For the first seven-eighths of its existence, there were no chordates of any kind, not even the simplest, living anywhere.

chordates 脊索动物

(2,492 words)

Unit 8 Earth and Space Science

❶ Recall

Answer the following questions with the information from the passage.

1. Who was notable for first attempting to estimate Earth's age?
2. What provided the solution both to the age of Earth and to the energy source of the Sun?
3. How did Edmond Halley justify his calculation for the Earth's age?
4. What is a quite simple and straight forward way of measuring the Earth's age?
5. According to the article, what are the elements that can be used to determine the age of Earth with considerable accuracy mentioned in this article?

❷ Interpret

Answer the following questions by analysing the passage.

6. Is sedimentation rate an accurate way of measuring the age of a fossil? Why?
7. According to Boltwood, how can we calculate the age of a rock?
8. According to the article, can you summarize how scientists calculate the age of Earth?

❸ Evaluate & Connect

Answer the following question by relating the passage to your own experience.

9. Why was there a conflict during the long process of discovering the age of Earth?

Science and Technology

Synopsis

科学技术是第一生产力,那么我们该如何理解科学技术及其影响呢?科学是人类在长期认识世界和改造世界的过程中所积累起来的知识体系;技术是指人类根据生产实践经验和应用科学原理而发展成的各种工艺操作方法和技能以及物化的各种生产手段和物质装备。这是两个概念,虽属不同范畴,却有着密不可分的联系。科学是技术的理论指导,但没有技术,科学对生产就没有实际意义。科学技术使不可能成为可能,使可能变得更快更好。科学技术的革新能极大地丰富人们的生活并带来极大的便利。本单元 Text A 通过介绍人工智能解释了自动化预测对劳动力市场的影响;Text B 通过介绍跟踪测量设备解释了科学技术进步给人类生活带来的影响。

Warm-up

Scan the QR code to see the stamps of some famous Chinese scientists. What are their research fields? Share some details you might know about them.

Text A

Background information

This article is extracted from the *Journal of Economic Perspectives,* which was published in 2019 and written by Ajay Agrawal, Joshua S. Gans, and Avi Goldfarb. This journal aims to fill the gap between the general interest press and academic economics journals. Recent advances in artificial intelligence are primarily driven by machine learning, a prediction technology. Prediction is useful because it is an input into decision-making. In order to appreciate the impact of artificial intelligence on the nature work, it is important to understand the relative roles of prediction and decision tasks. This article describes and provides examples of how artificial intelligence will affect labour, emphasizing differences between when the automation of prediction leads to automating decisions versus enhancing decision-making by humans.

Artificial Intelligence

—The Ambiguous Labor Market Impact of Automating Prediction
Ajay Agrawal, Joshua S. Gans, and Avi Goldfarb

Much of the public attention paid to artificial intelligence concerns its impact on jobs. Understanding this impact requires comprehending the capabilities of this technology. The majority of recent achievements in artificial intelligence are the result of advances in **machine learning**, a branch of computational statistics. Most of the concepts in standard machine learning textbooks are familiar to economists, like regression, maximum likelihood estimation, clustering, and nonparametric regression. Other techniques are just entering the **econometrician**'s toolkit: regression trees, neural networks, and **reinforcement** learning. Over the past decade or so, advances in computer speed, data collection, data storage, and **algorithm**s have led to substantial improvements in these techniques, such that their use for commercial applications is proceeding rapidly.

machine learning
　机器学习是人工智能的一个重要学科分支，是一门多领域交叉学科；在数据上通过算法总结规律模式，应用在新数据上。回归、最大似然估计、聚类和非参数回归都是机器学习中的概念。

econometrician 计量经济学家

reinforcement 强化

algorithm 算法

Machine learning does not represent an increase in artificial *general* intelligence of the kind that could substitute machines for all aspects of human cognition, but rather one particular aspect of intelligence: *prediction*. We define prediction in the statistical sense of using existing data to fill in missing information. As deep-learning pioneer **Geoffrey Hinton** (2016) said, "Take any old problem where you have to predict something and you have a lot of data, and deep learning is probably going to make it work better than the existing techniques."

Prediction is useful because it is an input into decision-making. Prediction has no value in the absence of a decision. In this sense, each prediction task is a perfect **complement** to a decision task. A prediction specifies the confidence of a probability associated with an outcome under conditions of uncertainty. As an input into decision-making under uncertainty, prediction is essential to many occupations, including service industries: teachers decide how to educate students, managers decide who to recruit and reward, and **janitor**s decide how to deal with a given mess. This wide breadth of application means that developments in artificial intelligence represent what Bresnahan and Trajtenberg (1995) called a "**general purpose technology**".

Prediction, however, is not the only element of a decision. Effective decision-making also requires collection and organization of data, the ability to take an action based on a decision, and the judgment to evaluate the **payoff**s associated with different outcomes. We characterize the decision task as distinct from the prediction task.

We examine four direct effects through which advances in prediction **technology may affect labour** in a task-based framework: 1) substituting **capital** for labour in prediction tasks; 2) automating decision tasks when automating prediction increases the relative returns to capital versus labour; 3) enhancing labour when **automating the prediction task** increases labour productivity in related decision tasks and thereby increases the relative returns to labour versus capital in those tasks; and 4) creating new decision tasks when automating prediction sufficiently reduces uncertainty as to enable new decisions that were not **feasible** before.

Geoffrey Hinton
杰弗里·辛顿（1947—），2018年图灵奖得主，英国皇家学会院士，加拿大皇家学会院士，美国国家科学院外籍院士，多伦多大学名誉教授。

complement 补充；补足

janitor 工友

general purpose technology 通用技术

payoff 结果；回报

technology may affect labour 技术会影响劳动方式。专家预计，在2025年人工智能将消灭8 500万个岗位，他们抢走了人类饭碗的同时，遵循着礼尚往来的原则，将创造9 700万个新岗位，但这却不是每个人都能捧得起的饭碗。

capital 资本

automating the prediction task 任务预测自动化

feasible 可行的

First, artificial intelligence may directly substitute capital for labour in prediction tasks. Some tasks, like demand forecasting, are already prediction tasks. Where humans currently perform these prediction tasks, they are increasingly replaced by artificial intelligence. At the same time, other tasks that were not historically viewed as prediction tasks are being transformed into prediction-oriented tasks as machine learning improves and the quality-adjusted cost of prediction decreases. Many parts of the **workflow** in human resources are being broken down into prediction tasks so that they can then be performed by artificial intelligence tools. For example, in the broad area of human resources, recruiting is the task of predicting—based on **resume**s, cover letters, LinkedIn profiles, and interview transcripts—which **subset** of applicants will perform best in the job. Promotion is the task of predicting which existing employees will perform best in a higher-level position. And **retention** is the task of predicting which star employees are most likely to leave and which of the available **incentive** options could most effectively be employed to encourage them to stay.

Second, when automated prediction can increase the relative returns to capital versus labour in **complementary** decision tasks, it can lead to the complete automation of a complementary decision task. For example, human reaction times are slower than those for machines. The returns to a machine predicting a potential car accident a few seconds or even **a fraction of a second** before a human would predict the accident is higher when the response time of the machine is faster. Thus, automating the prediction task increases the returns to also automating certain decision tasks associated with vehicle control. Sometimes, the artificial intelligence is able to make better predictions than a human could because it has access to different data, such as **feed**s from cameras, **RADAR**, and **LIDAR** around a car. Once the prediction task is automated, it increases the returns to automating some of the complementary tasks, such as those associated with vehicle control.

Third, automating the prediction task, in some cases, may have no impact on the **productivity of capital** performing a complementary task but may increase the **productivity of labour**. For example,

workflow 工作流程

resume 简历

subset 子集；小组

retention 保留

incentive 激励

complementary 补充的；辅助的

a fraction of a second 几分之一秒

feed 提供的信息

RADAR and LIDAR 雷达和激光雷达

productivity of capital 资本的生产力

productivity of labour 劳动生产力

ODS Medical developed a way of **transform**ing brain surgery for cancer patients. Previously, a surgeon would remove a **tumour** and surrounding **tissue** based on previous imaging (say, an MRI scan). However, to be certain all **cancerous** tissue is removed, surgeons frequently end up removing more brain matter than necessary. The ODS Medical device, which resembles a connected pen-like camera, uses artificial intelligence to predict whether an area of brain tissue has cancer cells or not. Thus, while the operation is taking place, the surgeon can obtain an immediate recommendation as to whether a particular area should be removed. By predicting with more than 90% accuracy whether a cell is cancerous, the device enables the surgeon to reduce both type I errors (removing noncancerous tissue) and type II errors (leaving cancerous tissue). The effect is to **augment** the labour of brain surgeons. Put simply, given a prediction, human decision-makers can in some cases make more **nuanced** and improved choices.

The fourth and final type of direct impact of artificial intelligence on labour happens when automated prediction sufficiently reduces uncertainty as to enable new decision tasks that did not exist before. The new tasks can be performed by capital or labour, depending on the relative costs of each. Some tasks that are not economically **viable** when uncertainty is high become viable as prediction technology reduces the level of uncertainty. This relates to the **reinstatement** force in Acemoglu and Restrepo where a freeing up of labour as a result of automation increases the returns to technologies that use labour for new tasks. At this early stage in the development and use of machine learning, there are a few **tangible** examples of new tasks that have already arisen because of recent advances in prediction technology.

The interaction of these four forces determines the net *direct* effect of cheaper quality-adjusted predictions on labour demand. There are also *indirect* effects: as some tasks become more efficient, demand for **upstream** and downstream tasks might change. For example, an artificial intelligence that automates translation on an online trading platform significantly enhances international trade. The application of this technology not only affects translators, but also the labour involved upstream and downstream on both sides of the trade.

transform 改变；转换
tumour 肿瘤
tissue（细胞）组织
cancerous 癌变的

augment 提高；增强
nuanced 细微的

viable 可行的

reinstatement 恢复；复原

tangible 有形的；真实的

upstream 上游

For individual workers, the relative importance of these forces will depend on the degree to which **the core skill they bring to their job** is predicated on prediction. Workers whose core skill is something other than prediction, such as the brain surgeon described above, may find that automated prediction enhances the value of their occupation. On the other hand, workers whose core skill is prediction, such as human resource workers who **screen** resumes, may find the value of their occupation diminished.

In our work with **the Creative Destruction Lab** at the University of Toronto, looking systematically at several hundred artificial intelligence **startup**s in the last few years, we have found that these firms often discuss how their technology will affect labour markets in specific occupations through substitution, complementarity, and demand expansion. We have seen very few companies building unambiguously labour-replacing technologies.

Overall, we cannot assess the net effect of artificial intelligence on labour as a whole, even in the short run. Instead, most applications of artificial intelligence have multiple forces that impact jobs, both increasing and decreasing the demand for labour. The net effect is an empirical question and will vary across applications and industries.

Automating prediction tasks

In this section, we describe examples that highlight substitution of human prediction by machine prediction in real-world **application**s.

Prediction in legal services

A number of artificial intelligence applications substitute capital for labour by automating prediction tasks in legal work, while still leaving the decision tasks to the human lawyer. We describe two examples.

Kira Systems uses artificial intelligence technology to scan contracts and summarize relevant content. This may involve predicting which party in a particular **lease** agreement is liable for what actions or expenses, or it may involve scanning all of the contracts signed by a firm to predict which ones would be impacted if that firm were involved in a **merger or acquisition**. It is still up to human lawyers to make the decisions (as regulation requires), but

---

the core skill they bring to their job
从业者的核心技能：如果某职业从业者的核心技能能在很大程度上被人工智能的预测能力替代，那么该职业从业者的技能将不再是不可或缺的。

screen 审查，筛选

the Creative Destruction Lab
创新颠覆实验室成立于2012年，总部位于加拿大排名第一的多伦多大学罗特曼管理学院。它擅长把一个学术领域内的科学想法或专利技术，转换为有竞争力的科技企业。

startup 新兴公司

application
应用，应用程序

Kira Systems
合同审查和分析的机器学习软件系统

lease 租赁

merger or acquisition
合并或收购

Kira's technology predicts the relevance of clauses and information in a fraction of the time it would take a lawyer or **paralegal**.

In addition, artificial intelligence technology is being used to predict likely judicial outcomes based on earlier legal judgments. Blue J Legal's artificial intelligence scans tax law and decisions to provide firms with predictions of their tax liability. As one example, tax law is often ambiguous on how income should be classified. At one extreme, if someone trades **securities** multiple times per day and holds securities for a short time period, then the profits are likely to be classified as **business income**. In contrast, if trades are rare and assets are held for decades, then profits are likely to be classified by the courts as **capital gains**. Currently, a lawyer who takes on a case collects the specific facts, conducts research on past judicial decisions in similar cases, and makes predictions about the case at hand. Blue J Legal uses machine learning to predict the outcome of new **fact scenarios** in tax and employment law cases. In addition to a prediction, the software provides a "case finder" that identifies the most relevant cases that help generate the prediction.

Prediction in driving

The potential for mass adoption of fully autonomous vehicles generates headlines, but prediction technology is already changing driving in a number of ways that do not replace human drivers with machines.

For example, vehicle manufacturers use artificial intelligence to warn drivers about **imminent** risks like "there is probably a car in your **blind spot**" or "there is likely a **pedestrian** behind your car" in the form of a beep or blinking light. The machine provides the prediction, but the driver is still responsible for the decision of whether to stop, turn, or proceed.

Vehicle **maintenance schedul**ing is another prediction problem. Decades ago, Rust (1987) developed **an empirical model** of Harold Zurcher, who was the **superintendent** of maintenance at the Madison (Wisconsin) Metropolitan Bus Company. Using statistical predictions of Zurcher's decisions, the model could be used to substitute for his predictions about when buses would break down. Today, advances in

---

paralegal 律师助理

security 证券

business income 营业收入

capital gains 资本收益

fact scenarios 事实场景

imminent 临近的

blind spot 视线盲区

pedestrian 行人

maintenance 维修；保养
schedule 计划；安排
an empirical model 经验模型
superintendent 主管人；负责人

sensors and prediction algorithms have led to many new products that predict when a vehicle will break down and thus inform the decision of whether to bring a vehicle in for maintenance.

Finally, prediction is changing commercial driving by providing effective predictions of the most efficient route between two locations at any given time. Perhaps the most dramatic example is the case of London taxicabs. For decades, earning a taxi license in London meant acquiring "The Knowledge", which involved learning the location of every address in London as well as the shortest route between any two addresses. To pass the resulting test took two to four years of study with the help of specialist training schools. But now, best-route prediction apps like Waze deliver "The Knowledge" to any driver with a smartphone, which is part of what enables **ride-sharing services** such as Uber to compete with London taxis. Although the skill of London **cabbies** did not diminish, their competitive advantage was seriously **erode**d by artificial intelligence.

Predictions in email responses

Composing an **email response** can be **formulate**d as a prediction problem. Google developed Smart Reply for its email service, Gmail, using artificial intelligence to scan incoming emails and predict possible responses. Smart Reply doesn't automate sending the email response but rather predicts possible responses and provides the user with three suggestions. In 2018, within weeks of Google **rolling out** Smart Reply as a default setting for all of its 1.4 billion active Gmail accounts, 10% of all Gmail responses sent were generated by Smart Reply (as reported by Marcelis and MacMillan 2018). This saves the user the time of composing a response in cases where one of the three predicted replies are sufficient. However, the user must still decide whether to send a predicted response or to compose one directly.

In some cases, this kind of artificial intelligence **implementation** might lead to a setting where a worker must still apply judgment about the benefits and costs of a particular decision before deciding or taking an action; in others, it might automate the full decision.

To understand how drafting email might affect different types of jobs differently, we turn to the **O*NET** database. Sponsored by

---

ride-sharing service 共享乘车服务

cabby 出租车司机

erode 削弱；侵蚀

email response 回复邮件

formulate 表达

roll out 推出

implementation 实施

O*NET 一项由美国劳工部组织发起开发的职位分析系统，该系统吸收了多种职位分析问卷的优点，目前已经取代职业名称词典，成为美国广泛应用的职位分析工具。

the US Department of Labor through a **grant** to the North Carolina Department of Commerce, O*NET offers detailed descriptions of the tasks involved in almost 1,000 occupations.	grant 拨款
This data includes a task described as "Prepare responses to correspondence containing routine inquiries." The job of **Executive Assistants** includes this task, along with eight other occupations: Correspondence Clerks, Tellers, Receptionists and Information Clerks, License Clerks, Legal Secretaries, Insurance Policy Processing Clerks, Medical Secretaries, and Loan Interviewers and Clerks. Executive Assistants would typically draft possible responses for someone else to decide whether or not to send, and so a system like Gmail's Smart Reply fully automates the Executive Assistant's decision. In the other jobs, the worker might make use of this technology but still retain the decision task of what to ultimately send. So in the former case, the artificial intelligence replaces labour, while in the latter case it enhances labour. (2, 392 words)	Executive Assistant 行政助理

❶ Recall

Answer the following questions with the information from the passage.

1. How is prediction defined in machine learning? Why is prediction useful and in which occupation?
2. What is essential to effective decision-making?
3. What idea does the ODS Medical example demonstrate?
4. What is the indirect effect of cheaper quality-adjusted predictions on labour demand?

❷ Interpret

Answer the following questions by analysing the passage.

5. How can we understand the effects of AI on labour?
6. Why does AI "prediction" matter? Can you give some examples?

Evaluate & Connect

Answer the following questions by relating the passage to your own experience.

7. Prediction tasks are gradually done more by AI, therefore many people are losing their jobs. How do you understand the relationship between unemployment and Sci &Tech progress?

8. In Paragraph 12, the writers say, "these firms often discuss how their technology will affect labour markets in specific occupations through substitution, complementarity, and demand expansion." How does technology affect your study life at present?

Text B

Background Information

This article is extracted from *Technology Review* published by the Massachusetts Institute of Technology in 2011. *Technology Review* is a magazine which introduces the latest technologies. The author Emily Singer is a senior editor for the magazine who writes about the brain and other strange natural phenomena. This article "explores new tools and trends in self-tracking, a growing movement in which people monitor various personal metrics in order to make more informed choices about living a healthier and more productive life".

The Measured Life

Emily Singer

Do you know how much REM sleep (快速眼动睡眠或主动睡眠) you got last night? New types of devices that monitor activity, sleep, diet, and even mood could make us healthier and more productive.

On a quiet Wednesday night in April, an unusual group has assembled in **a garage turned hacker studio nestle**d in a student-dominated neighbourhood outside Boston. Those gathered here—mostly in their 20s or 30s and mostly male—are united by a deep interest in themselves. They have come to share the results of their latest self-experiments: monthlong tests of the Zeo, a consumer device designed to analyse sleep.

The group is part of a rapidly growing movement of **fitness buffs, techno-geeks**, and patients with **chronic conditions** who **obsessively** monitor various personal **metrics**. At the centre of the movement is a loosely organized group known as the Quantified Self, whose members are driven by the idea that collecting detailed data can help them make better choices about their health and behaviour. In meetings held all over the world, self-trackers discuss how they use a combination of traditional spreadsheets, an expanding selection

---

a garage turned hacker studio 一个由车库改造成的黑客工作室

nestle 位处；坐落（于安全、隐蔽之处）

fitness buffs, techno-geeks 健身爱好者、科技极客

chronic conditions 慢性疾病

obsessively 痴迷地

metrics 衡量指标

of smart-phone apps, and various consumer and custom-built devices to monitor patterns of food intake, sleep, fatigue, mood, and heart rate.

Of course, **self-tracking** is not new. Many athletes have been **meticulously** monitoring personal metrics for decades. And some people with chronic conditions such as migraines, diabetes, and allergies have done the same in an effort to **shed light on** how daily habits may influence their symptoms. But new consumer tools have made self-tracking both simpler and more rigorous, generating reams of data that can be scrutinized for patterns and clues. The new devices, along with the increasing ease of sharing data with other users through social-networking sites, mean that more and more people are finding it useful to quantify their lives. The Zeo, a $199 device based on technology that until recently required the services of a trained technician, makes it easy for users to track their sleep cycles. The device consists of a soft head-band with a fabric sensor that wirelessly transmits **EEG** data to a bedside monitor. A programmable alarm clock wakes the wearer at the **optimal** phase of sleep. And each night's data can be uploaded to a computer, where users can study how their sleep is affected by environmental factors such as weather, light, and more.

Sanjiv Shah, a longtime **insomniac** who participates in the Boston group, believes that wearing orange-tinted glasses for several hours before bed makes it easier for him to fall asleep. (The theory is that the orange tint blocks blue light, which has been shown in both human and animal studies to influence **circadian rhythms**.) To quantify the effects, he used not only the Zeo but also a thumb-size device called the Fitbit, which incorporates an **accelerometer** that measures movement, and a camera trained on his bed to record his sleep for a month. His results: without the glasses, he took an average of 28 minutes to fall asleep, but with them he took only four.

The experiment has an obvious flaw: Shah knows when he is wearing the glasses, and he believes they work, so the **placebo effect** could be responsible for their success. Matt Bianchi, a neurologist at Massachusetts General Hospital who spoke at the **get-together**, says no large-scale studies have shown that orange glasses improve

sleep. (By the end of the evening, plans for a group experiment to test the technique were under way.) But self-trackers say the idea of reproducing the results in scientific tests **misses the point**. The glasses clearly work for Shah. And an $8 pair of plastic glasses is certainly preferable to sleep drugs as a way to gain that benefit.

As Gary Wolf, a journalist and cofounder of the Quantified Self, puts it, "It's a trial that begins with one very important person: yourself."

Self-hacking heaven

Over Memorial Day weekend, approximately 400 hackers, programmers, designers, engineers, and health-care professionals gathered at the Computer History Museum, in the **tech mecca** of Mountain View, California, for the first annual Quantified Self conference. Attendees showed off fitness monitors, apps to gather and display data, and even a set of **sticker sensors** with **embed**ded accelerometers to detect movement, which are designed to be stuck on toothbrushes, water bottles, or a dog's leash.

Standing out in the crowd was Alex Gilman, a researcher at Fujitsu Laboratories of America, who **amble**d down the main hall with a bag **slung** over his shoulder. A tangle of wires **sprout**ing from it led to monitors on different parts of his body: a white plastic ear clip, which measured his **blood oxygen** levels; **a blood pressure cuff** around his arm; and a combination heart rate monitor, **EKG**, **temperature gauge**, and accelerometer strapped to his chest. The bag itself held a prototype device designed to gather and **synchronize** the data from all those sensors and analyse it with the help of new **algorithm**s.

The devices are a taste of the not-so-distant future, when the monitoring tools now typical of a hospital's **intensive-care unit** will be transformed into wearable **gadget**s that are unobtrusive and effortless to use. Gilman's **chest strap** is from a company called Zephyr, which has traditionally made equipment to track the physiology of military personnel and emergency workers during stressful situations. Zephyr is developing simplified consumer versions of its products; the latest one tracks motion, heart rate, and

---

miss the point 没抓住重点

tech mecca 科技圣地

sticker sensors 贴纸传感器
embed 嵌入

amble 慢跑；缓行
sling 挂；吊
sprout 涌现出；出现
blood oxygen 血氧
a blood pressure cuff 血压袖带
EKG 心电图
temperature gauge 温度计
synchronize 同步
algorithm 算法；计算程序
intensive-care unit 重症监护室
gadget 小工具
chest strap 胸带

respiration and includes software to assess the user's fitness level. The blood pressure cuff and the clip to measure blood oxygen, which come from different manufacturers, are still too **bulky** to incorporate into consumer devices. The data, however, can be integrated into a single online **dashboard** with the help of Zephyr software.

The new generation of devices rely on inexpensive, low-power wireless **transceiver**s that can automatically send data to the wearer's cell phone or computer. Compared with the limited snapshot of health that is captured during an annual visit to the doctor's office, these tools and techniques could reveal the measures of someone's health "in context, and with a much richer resolution," says Paul Tarini, a senior program officer at the Robert Wood Johnson Foundation, which donated $64,000 to help the Quantified Self group create a guide to self-tracking tools.

Wearable sensors that measure vital signs such as blood pressure and heart rhythm **around the clock** could lead to applications we haven't thought of yet, says cardiologist Eric Topol, director of the Scripps Institute for Translational Medicine. Perhaps they could help people get a handle on health concerns such as headaches or fatigue, which don't qualify as diseases but can have a huge effect on quality of life. "People often get **light-headed** in daily activities," Topol says. "Is that symptom linked to an abnormal heart rhythm? Are headaches linked to abnormally high blood pressure?"

At the Quantified Self conference, the museum's walls were lined with posters describing personalized dashboards and other apps for collecting and **aggregat**ing data. But tools for analysing the data are much harder to come by. That's why Gilman and collaborators at Fujitsu built the device in his shoulder bag. One application they've developed is a way to use **time-stamped** raw data from wearable blood pressure monitors to make sure readings aren't taken when the user is active, which can yield misleading results. The new software tells the device to calculate blood pressure only when another monitor reveals that the wearer has been sitting still, as indicated by a steady heart rate.

The Fujitsu researchers are especially excited about using information collected **instantaneously** from the EKG to calculate

---

bulky 庞大的；笨重的

dashboard 仪表板

transceiver 无线电收发两用机

around the clock 24 小时；全天候

light-headed 头晕的

aggregate 汇总

time-stamped 有时间标记的

instantaneously 瞬时地

heart rate **variability**, **a well-validated indicator of stress**. Taking a reading with previous instruments requires the subject to stand or sit still for several minutes, says Dave Marvit, vice president of the Connected Information Innovation Centre at Fujitsu Laboratories of America. That makes it difficult to monitor stress as people go about their daily lives. Recently, Marvit tested the algorithm while moving naturally during an online game of speed chess. A graph charting his stress level in real time showed a **spike** as he contemplated a move to **throw off** his opponent's strategy, and a drop as he relaxed with the satisfaction of winning the game. "Seeing the physiological consequences of the mental state makes it much more real," he says. "It's much more interesting to measure stress while you're living your life than when you're standing still."

Better medicine

Perhaps the most interesting consequences of the self-tracking movement will come when its **adherent**s merge their findings into databases. The Zeo, for example, gives its users the option of making anonymized data available for research; the result is a database orders of magnitude larger than any other **repository** of information on sleep stages. Given that the vast majority of our knowledge about sleep—including the idea that eight hours is optimal—comes from highly controlled studies, this type of database could help to redefine healthy sleep behaviour. Sleep patterns may be much more variable than is currently thought. Zeo researchers have already found that women get less **REM** sleep than men and are now analysing whether the effect of aging on sleep differs by sex. The database is obviously biased, given that it is limited to people who bought the Zeo; those people are mostly men, with ample income and presumably some sleep-related concerns. But the sample is still probably at least as diverse as the population of the typical sleep study. Bianchi, who studies a number of sleep disorders and is developing his own home sleep-tracking tool, says an individualized approach to the study of sleep may help shed light on its complexities. "I have become sceptical of sleep science and clinical trials, so I am very interested in what individuals have to say," he says.

There are plenty of reasons to believe that people sharing data

---

variability 变异性；浮动
a well-validated indicator of stress 有效的压力指标

spike 尖峰
throw off 摆脱

adherent 拥护者

repository 储存库

REM 快速眼动的

about themselves can produce powerful medical insights. Patient groups formed around specific diseases have been among the first to recognize the benefits to be derived from aggregating such information and sharing it.

In 2004, Alexandra Carmichael, a long-time **migraine** sufferer, identified **dairy and gluten** as the triggers for her headaches after extensively tracking her pain and correlating it with diet and other factors. Hoping to help others find relief from chronic pain, she founded CureTogether, a social-networking site where patients can list their symptoms, the treatments they have tried, and the results they've observed. Aggregating and analysing the information has begun to reveal broader trends. For example, Carmichael and other members of CureTogether found evidence that people who experience **vertigo** with their migraines are four times more likely to see their pain increase than decrease if they take Imitrex, a migraine medication that constricts blood vessels. In the near term, new members to the site can use this information to help decide which treatments to try first. In the longer term, scientists studying migraines could explore this link more formally.

Such studies obviously lack the **rigor** of clinical trials, but they have their own advantages. Clinical trials usually impose **stringent** criteria, excluding people who have conditions or take medications other than the one being studied. But self-tracking studies often include such people, so their pool of participants may better reflect the actual patient population.

PatientsLikeMe, a social-networking site that provides users with tools to track their health status and communicate with other patients, has gathered a wealth of data on its 105,000 members. (The site makes money by **anonymiz**ing the data and selling it to **pharmaceutical** companies and other customers.) In 2008, after a small Italian study published in the Proceedings of the National Academy of Sciences suggested that **lithium** could delay the progression of **ALS**, or Lou Gehrig's disease, a small group of the ALS patients on PatientsLikeMe began taking the drug, and the company **rolled out** a number of tools to help them track their symptoms, their respiratory capacity, their **dosage** and blood levels

migraine 偏头痛

dairy and gluten 乳制品和麸质

vertigo 眩晕

rigor 严谨

stringent 严格的

anonymize 使匿名化

pharmaceutical 制药的

lithium 锂

ALS 肌萎缩性脊髓侧索硬化症

roll out 推出

dosage 剂量

of lithium, and any side effects they observed. Because the patients had collected so much data on themselves before starting the drug, researchers could analyse how their symptoms changed in the 12 months before they began taking it as well studying any changes that came after—something that's not possible in the typical clinical trial. The company published a study based on its data in April. The drug, unfortunately, was found to have no effect.

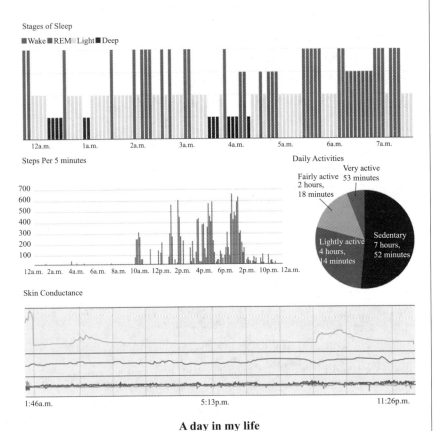

A day in my life

The graphs above illustrate a day in my life as documented by several of the devices that are now available to track everything from sleep to activity to stress. The top graph charts my sleep as recorded by the Zeo, revealing how many times I woke during the night. The middle section outlines the Fitbit's account of the number of steps I took over the course of the day (left) and the time I spent sedentary and mildly, moderately, or highly active. The results highlight how activity levels drop at work, even compared with evenings at home. The bottom graph shows data recorded by the Q sensor, from Affectiva, which detects skin conductance (top line), a measure related to stress, excitement, and activity. To help interpret the meaning of changes in conductance, the device also measures skin temperature (middle line) and movement (bottom lines). —Emily Singer

The growing **availability** of new monitoring devices and the increasing **sophistication** of social networks promise to make self-tracking much more powerful than it was when patients who wanted to monitor their own conditions were limited to standard spreadsheets and daily logs. "We see the potential to change the power **dynamics** in health care," says the Robert Wood Johnson Foundation's Tarini. People could take far more responsibility for monitoring their own health. The concept of personalized medicine could change as well; rather than relying on pharmaceutical companies that have little **incentive** to individualize treatments, patients could simply try different interventions and record how their physiological signs and symptoms change in response.

Of course, it remains to be seen whether a movement rooted in individual experimentation can **scale up** in ways that will affect public health. Even if it has the potential to do so, incorporating findings of this type into the health-care system is likely to be an enormous challenge. When you start with information from a study of one person, says Tarini, "the system doesn't have a way of determining what should be explored further." And because many of the new tools for tracking are aimed at consumers rather than the medical market, they have not undergone the rigorous testing required of medical devices. Still, Tarini is optimistic. "We have the opportunity to explore a whole new set of information," he says. "That has the potential to teach us a lot about health care."

The big payoff

The early adopters of self-tracking are often odd. In one breakout session at the May conference, a group earnestly discussed the results of their experiments. Standing on one leg for eight minutes a day helped one person sleep. Eating butter helped another think better. One had logged every line of computer code he'd written for a decade. But there is a far more **pragmatic** side to the movement, too. Across the building from the butter eater, another group, made up mostly of entrepreneurs, discussed business models for selling self-tracking apps and devices.

The favoured strategy of the moment is to weave together self-tracking tools with social networks and gaming, using the lessons

---

availability 可利用性
sophistication 复杂度

dynamics 动力

incentive 激励

scale up 放大；增大

pragmatic 实用的

of behavioural economics to keep users motivated enough to meet any health goals they've set for themselves. "We want to create an engaging device that makes people want to make better health choices," says Julie Wilner, product director at Basis, a **startup** developing a new watch laden with sensors. "We do that by tracking data and showing it on the Web and on mobile devices, and by sharing it with friends."

startup 新兴公司

Withings, a French company that makes wireless scales and blood pressure monitors, gives users the option of **tweet**ing their weight, with the goal of adding social pressure to make people **stick to** a diet. (Only a small percentage of users employ that feature, and the vast majority of them are men. The company is also experimenting with delaying **readings** from the scale. That way, the user may be less likely to get discouraged on a bad day and stop weighing herself.) And Green Goose, the startup developing the sensor-equipped stickers for household objects, plans to create a game based on personal health goals, awarding points whenever the user walks the dog or takes vitamins.

tweet 用推特发布

stick to 坚持；遵循

readings（测量仪器上的）读数

Yet even as startups plot how to profit from the trend, the people behind the self-tracking movement have a very different **mind-**set— and very different goals. "I find that the most interesting tools are those that give us the chance to reflect on who we are," says Wolf, the Quantified Self founder. The problems self-tracking tries to solve, he says, are important to everyone's life: "How to eat, how to sleep, how to learn, how to work, how to be happy."

mind-set 思维模式

❶ Recall

Answer the following questions with the information from the passage.

1. Why did this unusual group assemble in Boston?
2. What are the members of the Quantified Self group driven by?
3. What is the obvious flaw of Sanjiv Shah's experiment about the effects of orange-tinted glasses?
4. What will the new generation of self-tracking devices in the not-so-distant future be like according to the author?

5. What's the function of the bag slung over Gilman's shoulder (Paragraph 8)?
6. What are the advantages of self-tracking studies compared with clinical trials?

II Interpret

Answer the following question by analysing the passage.

7. "We see the potential to change the power dynamics in health care," says Paul Tarini of the Robert Wood Johnson Foundation. What makes him see the potential? What changes could it bring to health care? What do you think of these changes?

III Evaluate & Connect

Answer the following questions by relating the passage to your own experience.

8. The problems self-tracking tries to solve, he says, are important to everyone's life: "How to eat, how to sleep, how to learn, how to work, how to be happy." Have you ever used self-tracking apps or devices? If yes, what are they, and what are their functions? What do you think of them? If no, what kind of apps or devices do you wish to use? What functions do you expect from it?

9. The present self-tracking devices are made based on western medicine. Suppose that one device is made based on the pulse-feeling of traditional Chinese medicine (中医切脉), how will it be like in your imagination?

Science: Past and Future

Synopsis

  知史鉴今，观照未来。这足以表明历史对于预知未来的重要性。同理，科学的历史是科学发展之母。我们知道，科学创新与发展是推动现代社会进步的原动力。治愈疾病，载人航空，乡村振兴，这些都离不开科学的持续发展。可以说，科学发展是推进中国式现代化的强大基石。毋庸置疑，探究科学的历史与未来两者之间的关系显得尤为迫切。本单元 Text A 阐明现代生物学的发展离不开达尔文奠基者的影响；Text B 在着重说明想象力、人类需求和提出新问题等诸因素对推动科学创新和发展至关重要的同时，还探讨了科学发展的趋势并展望未来。

Warm-up

Throughout history, there have been a lot of famous sayings about science at home and abroad, which impart wisdom and sage advice. Below are a few examples:

Science wins when its wings are uninhibited with imagination. —Michael Faraday (Britain)

Surprise is the seed of science. —Thomas Alva Edison (America)

Science is for those who are studious. —Joseph Roux (France)

Scientific inspiration is not from idling. —Hua Luogeng (China)

...

1) Think of more sayings about science.

2) Choose one saying and share your own interpretation.

3) In *Of Studies*, Frances Bacon states that histories make men wise. What wisdom can you obtain from these historical sayings?

Text A

Background information

This excerpt is taken from the book *The End of Science—Facing the Limits of Knowledge in the Twilight of the Scientific Age* by John Horgan in 2015. The book was first published in 1996, and became a bestseller that was translated into 13 languages. John Horgan received a B.A. in English from Columbia University's School of General Studies in 1982 and an M.S. from Columbia's School of Journalism in 1983. Horgan was a full-time staff writer at *Scientific American* from 1986 to 1997, when the magazine fired him due to a dispute over his first book, *The End of Science*, which reveals his pessimistic outlook on the future of science. Eight years later, Horgan wrote a few freelance articles for *Scientific American*, notably "The Forgotten Era of Brain Chips". From 2010–2022, he churned out hundreds of opinion pieces for the magazine's online edition. Horgan has also written for *The New York Times*, *Wall Street Journal*, *National Geographic*, *Washington Post* and so on. His subsequent books include *The Undiscovered Mind*, *Rational Mysticism*, *The End of War*, *Mind-Body Problems*, *Pay Attention* and *My Quantum Experiment*.

The End of Evolutionary Biology

John Horgan

No other field of science is as burdened by its past as is evolutionary biology. It **reeks of** what the literary critic **Harold Bloom** called the anxiety of influence. The discipline of evolutionary biology can be defined to a large degree as the ongoing attempt of Darwin's intellectual descendants to **come to terms with** his overwhelming influence. Darwin based his theory of natural selection, the central component of his vision, on two observations. First, plants and animals usually produce more offspring than their environment can sustain. Second, these offspring differ slightly from their parents and from each other. Darwin concluded that each organism, in its struggle to survive long enough to reproduce, competes either directly or indirectly with others of its species. Chance plays a role in the

---

reek of 充满

Harold Bloom
哈罗德·布鲁姆（1930—2019），美国著名文学家，"耶鲁学派"批评家和文学理论家，代表作为《影响的焦虑：一种诗歌理论》（1937）。

come to terms with
接受；适应；对……妥协

survival of any individual organism, but nature will favour, or select, those organisms whose variations make them slightly more fit, that is, more likely to survive long enough to reproduce and pass on those adaptive variations to their offspring.

Darwin could only guess what **gives rise to** the all-important variations between generations. *On the Origin of Species*, first published in 1859, mentioned a proposal set forth by the French biologist **Jean-Baptiste Lamarck**, that organisms could pass on not only inherited but also acquired characteristics to their heirs. For example, the constant **craning** of a giraffe to reach leaves high in a tree would alter its **sperm** or egg so that its offspring would be born with longer necks. But Darwin was clearly uncomfortable with the idea that adaptation is self-directed. He preferred to think that variations between generations are random, and that only under the pressure of natural selection do they become adaptive and lead to evolution.

Unbeknownst to Darwin, during his lifetime an Austrian monk named **Gregor Mendel** was conducting experiments that would help refute Lamarck's theory and vindicate Darwin's intuition. Mendel was the first scientist to recognize that natural forms can be subdivided into **discrete** traits, which are transmitted from one generation to the next by what Mendel termed *hereditary particles* and are now called genes. Genes prevent the blending of traits and thereby preserve them. The recombination of genes that takes place during sexual reproduction, together with occasional genetic mistakes, or **mutations**, provides the variety needed for natural selection to work its magic.

Mendel's 1868 paper on breeding pea plants went largely unnoticed by the scientific community until the turn of the century. Even then, Mendelian genetics was not immediately **reconciled with** Darwin's ideas. Some early geneticists felt that genetic mutation and sexual recombination might guide evolution along certain paths independently of natural selection. But in the 1930s and 1940s, **Ernst Mayr** of Harvard University and other evolutionary biologists **fused** Darwin's ideas with genetics into a powerful restatement of his

give rise to 引起；导致

Jean-Baptiste Lamarck 让·巴蒂斯特·拉马克（1744—1829），法国著名博物学家，生物进化论的奠基人，其进化思想对达尔文的自然选择学说产生深刻影响。

crane 伸长（脖子）

sperm 精子；精液

unbeknownst 不为所知的

Gregor Mendel 格里高尔·孟德尔（1822—1884），19世纪的奥地利僧侣和科学家，被誉为现代遗传学之父。他通过对豌豆植物的研究，发现了遗传规律，奠定了遗传学的基础。

discrete 分离的；个别的；互不相连的

mutation 变异；突变

be reconciled with 与……和解/妥协

Ernst Mayr 恩斯特·迈尔（1904—2005），出生于德国，20世纪杰出的演化生物学家，被誉为"20世纪的达尔文"。

fuse 融合；结合

theory, called the new synthesis, which affirmed that natural selection is the primary architect of biological form and diversity.

The discovery in 1953 of the structure of DNA—which serves as the blueprint from which all organisms are constructed—confirmed Darwin's intuition that all life is related, descended from a common source. Watson and Crick's finding also revealed the source of both continuity and variation that makes natural selection possible. In addition, **molecular** biology suggested that all biological phenomena could be explained in mechanical, physical terms.

That conclusion was by no means **foregone**, according to **Gunther Stent**. In *The Coming of the Golden Age*, he noted that prior to the unravelling of DNA's structure, some prominent scientists felt that the conventional methods and assumptions of science would prove inadequate for understanding heredity and other basic biological questions. The physicist **Niels Bohr** was the major proponent of this view. He contended that just as physicists had to cope with an uncertainty principle in trying to understand the behaviour of an **electron**, so would biologists face a fundamental limitation when they tried to **probe** living organisms too deeply:

> there must remain an uncertainty as regards the physical condition to which [the organism] is subjected, and the idea suggests itself that the minimal freedom we must allow the organism in this respect is just large enough to hide its ultimate secrets from us. On this view, the existence of life must be considered as a starting point in biology, in a similar way as the **quantum** of action, which appears as an irrational element from the point of view of classical mechanical physics, taken together with the existence of the elementary particles, forms the foundation of quantum mechanics.

Stent accused Bohr of trying to revive the old, **discredited** concept of vitalism, which holds that life stems from a mysterious essence or force that cannot be reduced to a physical process. But Bohr's vitalist vision has not been **borne out**. In fact, molecular biology has proved one of Bohr's own **dicta**, that science, when it is most successful, reduces mysteries to trivialities.

---

molecular 分子的

foregone conclusion
不可避免的结果；不容怀疑的东西

Gunther Stent
冈瑟·斯坦特（1924— ），出生于德国柏林，美国著名的分子生物学家和科学院院士，在分子生物学、神经生物学和科学哲学三个领域做出重要贡献。

Niels Bohr
尼尔斯·玻尔（1885—1962），丹麦物理学家、皇家科学院院士，1922年获得诺贝尔物理学奖。

electron 电子

probe 探究；探索

quantum 量子

discredited 不可信的

bear out 证实

dicta 格言；权威的断言

What can an ambitious young biologist do to make his or her mark in the post-Darwin, post-DNA era? One alternative is to become more Darwinian than Darwin, to accept Darwinian theory as a supreme insight into nature, one that cannot be transcended. That is the route taken by the arch-clarifier and reductionist **Richard Dawkins** of the University of Oxford. He has **honed** Darwinism into a fearsome weapon, one with which he obliterates any ideas that challenge his resolutely materialistic, non-mystical view of life. He seems to view the persistence of creationism and other anti-Darwinian ideas as a personal **affront**.

I met Dawkins at a gathering **convened** by his literary agent in Manhattan. He is an icily handsome man, with **predatory** eyes, a knife-thin nose, and **incongruously** rosy cheeks. He wore what appeared to be an expensive, custom-made suit. When he held out his finely veined hands to make a point, they quivered slightly. It was the tremor not of a nervous man, but of a finely tuned, high-performance competitor in the war of ideas: Darwin's **greyhound**.

As in his books, Dawkins in person **exuded** a supreme self-assurance. His statements often seemed to have an implied **preamble**: "As any fool can see..." An unapologetic atheist, Dawkins announced that he was not the sort of scientist who thought science and religion addressed separate issues and thus could easily coexist. Most religions, he contended, hold that God is responsible for the design and purpose evident in life. Dawkins was determined to **stamp out** this point of view. "All purpose comes ultimately from natural selection," he said. "This is the **credo** that I want to put forward."

Dawkins then spent some 45 minutes setting forth his ultra reductionist version of evolution. He suggested that we think of genes as little bits of software that have only one goal: to make more copies of themselves. **Carnations**, **cheetahs**, and all living things are just elaborate vehicles that these "copy-me programs" have created to help them reproduce. Culture, too, is based on copy-me programs, which Dawkins called **memes**. Dawkins asked us to imagine a book with the message: Believe this book and make your children believe it or when you die you will all go to a very unpleasant place called hell. "That's a very effective piece of copy-me code. Nobody is

---

Richard Dawkins
理查德·道金斯（1941—），英国著名演化生物学家、动物行为学家和科普作家，英国皇家科学院院士，牛津大学教授。

hone 磨砺；使更锋利（有效）

affront 冒犯；侮辱

convene 召集（会议）；召开

predatory 捕食性的；食肉的

incongruously 不协调地；不和谐地

greyhound 灰狗（一种猎犬）；录缇犬

exude 散发；洋溢；充分显露

preamble 序言；前言

stamp out 消除；根除

credo 信条；教义

carnation 康乃馨

cheetah 猎豹

meme 模因；文化基因

foolish enough to just accept the **injunction**, 'Believe this and tell your children to believe it.' You have to be a little more subtle and dress it up in some more elaborate way. And of course, we know what I'm talking about."

Dawkins then **fielded** questions from the audience, **a motley assortment of** journalists, educators, book editors, and other quasi-intellectuals. One listener was John Perry Barlow, a former Whole Earth hippie and occasional **lyricist** for the Grateful Dead who had **mutated into** a New Age cyber-prophet. Barlow, a **bearish** man with a red **bandanna** tied around his throat, asked Dawkins a long question having something to do with where information *really* exists.

Dawkins's eyes narrowed, and his nostrils **flared** ever so slightly as they caught the scent of **woolly-headedness**. Sorry, he said, but he did not understand the question. Barlow spoke for another minute or so. "I feel you are trying to get at something which interests you but doesn't interest me," Dawkins said and scanned the room for another questioner. Suddenly, the room seemed several degrees chillier.

Later, during a discussion about extraterrestrial life, Dawkins set forth his belief that natural selection is **a cosmic principle**; wherever life is found, natural selection has been at work. He **cautioned** that life cannot be too common in the universe, because thus far we have found no evidence of life on other planets in the solar system or elsewhere in the cosmos. Barlow bravely broke in to suggest that our inability to detect alien life-forms may stem from our perceptual inadequacies. "We don't know who discovered water," Barlow added meaningfully, "but we can be pretty sure it wasn't fish." Dawkins turned his **level** gaze on Barlow. "So you mean we're looking at them all the time," Dawkins asked, "but we don't see them?" Barlow nodded. "Yessss," Dawkins sighed, as if **exhaling** all hope of enlightening the unutterably stupid world.

Dawkins can be equally harsh with his fellow biologists, those who have dared to challenge the basic paradigm of Darwinism. He has argued, with devastating persuasiveness, that all attempts to modify or transcend Darwin in any significant way are **flawed**. He opened his 1986 book *The Blind Watchmaker* with the following **proclamation**: "Our existence once presented the greatest of all

---

injunction 禁令；命令；劝告

field 处理；回应

a motley assortment of 各种各样

lyricist 歌词作者

mutate into 变成

bearish 粗暴的；如熊的

bandanna 扎染印花大手帕

flare（鼻孔）张开

woolly-headedness 头脑不清；思考混乱

a cosmic principle 宇宙法则

caution 警告；告诫

level 平静的；冷静的

exhale 呼出；散发出

flawed 有瑕疵的；有缺陷的

proclamation 宣言

mysteries, but...it is a mystery no longer because it is solved. Darwin and Wallace solved it, though we shall continue to add footnotes to their solution for a while yet."

"There's always an element of rhetoric in those things," Dawkins replied when I asked him later about the footnotes remark. "On the other hand, it's a legitimate piece of rhetoric," in that Darwin did solve "the mystery of how life came into existence and how life has the beauty, the adaptiveness, the complexity it has." Dawkins agreed with Gunther Stent that all the great advances in biology since Darwin—Mendel's demonstration that genes come in discrete packages, Watson and Crick's discovery of the **double-helical** structure of DNA—**buttressed** rather than undermined Darwin's basic idea.

double-helical 双螺旋的

buttress 支持

Molecular biology has recently revealed that the process whereby DNA interacts with RNA and proteins is more complicated than previously thought, but the basic paradigm of genetics—DNA-based genetic transmission—is in no danger of collapsing. "What would be a serious reversal," Dawkins said, "would be if you could take a whole organism, a zebra on **the Serengeti Plain**, and allow it to acquire some characteristic, like learning a new route to the water hole, and have that backward encoded into the **genome**. Now if anything like that were to happen, I really would eat my hat."

the Serengeti Plain 塞伦盖蒂平原（坦桑尼亚地名）

genome 基因组；染色体组

There are still some rather large biological mysteries left, such as the origin of life, of sex, and of human consciousness. Developmental biology—which seeks to show how a single fertilized cell becomes a **salamander** or an **evangelist**—also raises important issues. "We certainly need to know how that works, and it's going to be very, very complicated." But Dawkins insisted that developmental biology, like molecular genetics before it, would simply fill in more details within the Darwinian paradigm.

salamander 火蜥蜴；蝾螈

evangelist 福音传道者

Dawkins was "**fed up**" with those intellectuals who argued that science alone could not answer ultimate questions about existence. "They think science is too arrogant and that there are certain questions that science has no business to ask, that traditionally have been of interest to religious people. As though they had any answers. It's one

fed up 厌烦

thing to say it's very difficult to know how the universe began, what **initiated** the big bang, what consciousness is. But if science has difficulty explaining something, there sure as hell is no one else who is going to explain it." Dawkins quoted, with great **gusto**, a remark by the great British biologist Peter Medawar that some people "'enjoy **wallowing** in a nonthreatening **squalor** of incomprehension.' I want to understand," Dawkins added fiercely, "and understanding means to me scientific understanding."

I asked Dawkins why he thought his message—that Darwin basically told us all we know and all we need to know about life—met with resistance not only from creationists or New Agers or philosophical **sophists**, but even from obviously competent biologists. "It may be I don't **get the point across** with sufficient clarity," he replied. But the opposite, of course, is more likely to be true. Dawkins gets his point across with utter clarity, so much so that he leaves no room for mystery, meaning, purpose—or for great scientific revelations beyond the one that Darwin himself gave us.

(2,102 words)

initiate 引发；发起

gusto 热情；兴致

wallow 沉溺；沉迷

squalor 肮脏；悲惨；卑劣；道德败坏

sophist 诡辩家；学者；哲学家

get... across 把……讲清楚

❶ Recall

Answer the following questions with the information from the passage.

1. According to Harold Bloom's anxiety of influence, who was the forefather of evolutionary biology?
2. Who put forward the proposal that organisms could pass on not only inherited but also acquired characteristics to their heirs?
3. What were genes called by Mendel?
4. What was Darwin's intuition that was confirmed by the discovery in 1953 of the structure of DNA?
5. What is the concept of vitalism?
6. Does Dawkins think science and religion can easily coexist?

II Interpret

Answer the following questions by analysing the passage.

7. At the very beginning of Paragraph 11, the author says, "Dawkins then spent some 45 minutes setting forth his ultra reductionist version of evolution." According to Dawkins, what does his ultra reductionist version of evolution mean?

8. What can you infer from the discussion about extraterrestrial life between Dawkins and Barlow in Paragraph 14?

III Evaluate & Connect

Answer the following question by relating the passage to your own experience.

9. Do you agree with those intellectuals who argue that science alone cannot answer ultimate questions about existence? Based on your own knowledge, try to elaborate your viewpoint.

Text B

Background Information

This present article is mainly about what the world of science will be like in 2040. It is an excerpt from Chapter 7 of the book *The Fabulous Future?: America and the World in 2040* edited by Gary Saul Morson and Morton Schapiro and published by Northwestern University Press in 2015. The author Mark A. Ratner (1942–), whose research area mainly covers molecular structure and properties, is a distinguished American chemist and Professor Emeritus at Northwestern University. In 1974, he was acclaimed as the "father of molecular-scale electronics".

Science Especially About the Future

Mark A. Ratner

The great Danish physicist and philosopher **Niels Bohr** is credited with saying, "Prediction is very difficult, especially about the future." In Denmark, this remark is usually attributed to Storm P, a creative newspaper cartoonist of the early twentieth century. When thinking about predicting or even imagining the scientific advances by the year 2040, it is wise to remember that these remarks came both from a physicist/philosopher and from a newsman/cartoonist. While the word "science" has its roots in the Greek word meaning "knowledge," much of science comes from the collaboration/conflict of knowledge and imagination. And it's almost certainly true that in 2015 our imagination of where science will be twenty-five years out is going to be incorrect, unimaginative, and wide of the mark. It is a challenge, and an opportunity to have fun—what *will* science be like in 2040?

Questions, answers, and more questions

Science is in the business of asking these questions. **I. I. Rabi** (another thoughtful Nobel Prize winner in physics) relates the story

---

Niels Bohr
　尼尔斯·玻尔（1885—1962），丹麦物理学家，丹麦皇家科学院院士，1922 年获诺贝尔物理学奖。

I. I. Rabi
　拉比（1898—1988），奥地利物理学家，20 世纪最杰出的科学家之一，1944 年获诺贝尔物理学奖。

that when he returned home from school, his mother didn't ask him what he had learned today but rather "did you ask a good question today?" Asking the right good questions, and answering them as best we can, is the **hallmark** of true science. And as humans we do question, and when we stop questioning, we stop learning. So it seems that the nature of the human being is going to result in vibrant, ongoing science four decades out, and far beyond.

hallmark 特点；标志

Another way of seeing is technology. When I **polled** my undergraduate students on what science is going to be like twenty-five years out, they wrote quite persuasively about the disappearance of computer screens, the **omnipresence** of communications, the biomedical devices that will make our lives far richer, self-driving and self-parking cars, and all the other advances that will certainly happen and will probably be **dwarfed** by other accomplishments of technology. But predicting technology twenty-five years out is even more **fraught** than doing that for science. Science depends on imagination, on experiment, and on the building of understanding. Technology is the powerful, lusty, productive, ungoverned love child of science and business. Advances in technology travel many roads, from the Edisonian approach of trying many things (which has now become, in slicked-up form, one of the ways of doing both molecular and materials discovery) to the computational data discovery and data mining that are one of the flavours of today. So our discussion here will exclude technology, because unlike science, it's not so much about asking questions as about anticipating, answering, and creating demands and interacting with the requirements and desires of people.

poll 对……进行民意调查

omnipresence 无所不在

dwarf 使相形见绌

fraught 令人担忧的

Why, how, and looking forward

The drivers of scientific inquiry have varied over the years. The **alchemists** were driven by desire both for riches and for ways to interfere with the mortality tables. Despite this, they contributed tremendously to the growth of modern chemistry. For roughly the last 150 years, the major drivers for science were a combination of military (Rumford, Heisenberg, Haber, and others), curiosity (Faraday, Hilbert, Einstein, etc.), and nutrition (Borlaug, Haber, Carver, et al.). A great deal of science came from simple need for **filthy lucre**: while it didn't pay very well in most cases, scientific

alchemist 炼金术士

filthy lucre 不义之财

endeavour was rewarded by the society, and some outstanding scientists could attain unimagined status—excellent scientists such as Lavoisier, Rutherford, Gibbs, Crick, Langmuir, and many others lived very well indeed.

  The foregoing list is entirely male and entirely white. This **homogeneity** has begun to change, with huge advantages both for the creativity of science and for the ability of science to explain the universe. The scientific workforce of 2015 is more diverse in every area than it has ever been before—gender, race, age, residence, and social standing are less determinative of scientific success. In 2040, the scientific workforce will be driven by curiosity, by the wish for reward, and by human needs. Human needs–driven science is already important (National Institutes of Health!), but it will be more so twenty-five years out, when (provided diplomacy keeps up with science) the world will, for the first time, no longer have hunger as a cause of death. Human needs involving health, creativity, leisure, longevity, and the opportunity to create, to enjoy, and to **savour** the best parts of life will be principal drivers for scientific exploration.

  In 2040 the interest in, and domination of, life sciences will be even greater than it is now. We will continue to seek understanding of biological processes, both synthetic and natural. One huge challenge in life science has to do with the enormous diversity that living creatures represent. This has generated a set of life sciences that are breathtaking in their breadth, depth, and importance. They are also **balkanized** in their rules and understandings.

  Mathematics has crucially important theorems and methodologies, going back to Newton and Leibniz and proceeding through Gauss, Hilbert, and many others. Physics has Newton's laws and Einstein's extension of them; it has the laws of **thermodynamics** (which it shares with chemistry) and the laws of quantum mechanics (which it shares with all the other sciences). Earth science has all of chemistry and physics to support it, in addition to the understandings of **Wegener** concerning continental drift that has dominated much of the evolution of and on the earth for the past few million years. Chemistry is the most **syncretic** and broad of all the sciences. It requires for its understanding all of the above, plus ideas and methods

---

homogeneity 同质性

savour 尽情享受；品尝；欣赏

balkanize 使割据

thermodynamics 热力学

Alfred Wegener 阿尔弗雷德·韦格纳（1880—1930），德国气象学家和地球物理学家，提出第一个完整的大陆漂移假说。

syncretic 融合的

such as **Faraday**'s laws for electrochemistry, the quantum and statistical mechanics of physics, polymer science, and many other themes gathered from the knowledge that humanity has developed since the Greeks.

But biology is different. Published in 2015, the wonderful compendium entitled *Molecular Biology of the Cell* (Alberts et al.) contains twenty-five chapters. Written by some of the true leaders in the life sciences, it describes issues ranging from antibodies to **zooplankton**. But overall integrating concepts and quantitative relationships are nearly lacking. Moreover, life science is more essentially **compartmentalized** than earth science, physics, chemistry, and others. The science required to understand the nervous system and the science required to understand **photosynthesis** are intrinsically different. DNA replication has little to do with kidney function; brain science and bone science rely on different interpretations of structure and behaviour.

In 2040, the quest for more general organizing principles in the biological sciences will have advanced substantially. In 2015, the wonderful ability to maintain understandings by a series of well-defined equations (the **cornerstone** of physics) fails to describe biological structure and dynamics. Even twenty-five years out, it is not clear that those understandings will have been completed in life science.

In 2015, we are aware of the existence of millions of **exoplanets** (planets circling stars that are not our sun), and it is probable that there are at least a million times (or a hundred million or a billion or...) that many. Certainly some of these planets have water on them, and the combination of the water and the sunlight, plus a **nitrogenous** atmosphere from historical times, strongly suggests that some sort of life might well have evolved on those planets. At some time in the future (unless the human inhabitants of Earth destroy it), there will be communication between Earth and one of these planets. That will be the most awesome (a word popular among young people in 2015) event in the history of humankind. Proof that we are not alone, that elsewhere in the universe there is life—and life that in some sense is akin to our own—would be the greatest news story ever, and it

Michael Faraday 迈克尔·法拉第（1791—1867），英国物理学家和化学家，也是著名的自学成才的科学家。

zooplankton 浮游动物

compartmentalize 划分；区分

photosynthesis 光合作用

cornerstone 基石；支柱

exoplanet（太阳系以外的）外部行星

nitrogenous 含氮的

would arise from **astrophysics**. This will eventually happen. With advances in radio astronomy and detection, as well as our knowledge of the existence of exoplanets, it could well happen by 2040. **Carl Sagan**, using the Drake equation and some reasonable assumptions, deduced in the twentieth century that there are thriving civilizations in our galactic neighbourhood. Making their acquaintance would be stupendous!

Some actual predictions

The late Irving Klotz, an articulate and distinguished faculty member in the Northwestern University Chemistry Department, was fond of saying of many scientists that they were "frequently in error, but never in doubt". Being in error—in an intelligent, creative, falsifiable, and combinative way—is a great accomplishment in science, and these predictions certainly demonstrate that.

Technology will continue, both unstopped and unstoppable. We will have universal connectivity among individuals worldwide, and we will have driverless cars. We may have fully renewable energy sources. We'll have instant daily diagnosis of diseases, life expectancy will exceed one hundred years, and we will probably have many more artificial components to our bodies than we do now. But these engineering accomplishments, though they will certainly change our lives (and probably mostly for the better) are not disruptive at the level of the great inventions of the past. Those included tonal music, evolution, the classification of animals and plants, calculus, relativity, thermodynamics, evolution, flight, the printing press, radio, the steam engine, fire, splitting atoms, **anaesthesia**, and quantum mechanics. But asking the right question is frequently the most important thing in science. New questions will be asked, and new conceptual breakthroughs—perhaps in a class with music, flight, and fire—will be born.

The growth of science is remarkable. It is estimated that more than 50% of all the scientists who ever lived were born after 1900. Indeed, the word "scientist" is relatively new—it was coined by **William Whewell** in 1833. In 2015, there are more scientists alive than there ever have been previously, and they are better supported by

---

astrophysics
天体物理学

Carl Sagan
卡尔·萨根（1934—1996），美国天文学家、天体物理学家、宇宙学家和科幻作家。

anaesthesia 麻醉

William Whewell
威廉·惠威尔（1794—1866），英国19世纪最著名的科学家之一，提出归纳法，倡导归纳科学。

government, by individuals, by companies, and by philanthropy. This could not possibly have been imagined when Michael Faraday was supposed to have said to Gladstone (who had asked what good would come from electricity), "Why, sir, there is every probability that you will soon be able to tax it."

The philosopher of science **Karl Popper** claimed that a true scientific fact had to be falsifiable—that is, such statements as "this is a happy onion" or "that rock is really distressed" are not scientific statements because they can't be disproven. Accordingly, it has become a norm in experimental science over the last century to publish results in open journals so that they can be reproduced or not. Quoting the *Economist* (October 13, 2013), "The idea that the same experiments always get the same results, no matter who performs them, is one of the cornerstones of science's claim to objective truth. If a systematic campaign of replication does not lead to the same results, then either the original research is flawed or the replications are. Either way, something is **awry**." The *Economist* goes on to say that because some experiments are extremely difficult, the statistics are difficult to understand, and there are huge expenditures involved in making observations or measurements. Falsification is no longer a significant activity. The *Economist* describes the current state of falsifiability as essentially irrelevant.

Bruce Alberts (the brilliant and prolific scientist mentioned earlier, who was both the editor of *Science* magazine and the president of the National Academy of Sciences) is quoted in the *Economist* as saying, "Scientists themselves... need to develop a value system where simply moving on from one's mistakes without publicly acknowledging them severely damages, rather than protects scientific reputation." The *Economist* finishes the discussion by saying that "this will not be easy. But if science is to stay on its tracks, and be worthy of the trust so widely invested in it, it may be necessary."

Science is done by people. Often these people are extremely careful and painstaking; more often, these people are only as careful and painstaking as they feel it is necessary to be. Mistakes are made, and in various fields of science those mistakes can be falsified quite

Karl Popper
卡尔·波普尔（1902—1994），出生于奥地利的一个犹太裔中产家庭，1976年当选英国皇家科学院院士，20世纪最著名的哲学家之一。

awry 歪的；出错的

Bruce Alberts
布鲁斯·艾伯茨（1938— ），美国科学院院士、生物化学和生物物理学系教授，《科学》杂志主编。

quickly—if a new molecule is made in a particular way and the preparation is published, other scientists can try to reproduce it—and if they can't, the originator almost certainly has made an error. The search for novelty in science and the nature of the support of scientific research guarantee that game-changing ideas will be examined but do not guarantee that these ideas can be falsified or will be examined from the viewpoint of falsification. So the definition of truth in science will be based on the acceptance by scientific peers and not whether the idea can be falsified.

Science is certainly a healthy and growing subculture within society. Per the National Science Board, the United States publishes more science and engineering articles than any other country, although the combined output of the European Union is larger than that of the United States. Asia's research article output is approaching **parity** with the United States and the European Union. Between 1997 and 2011, Asia's output more than doubled, led primarily by China. In 2011, China produced 11% of the world's science and engineering articles, more than any country except the United States. Publication of such papers shows no signs of stopping, but it eventually must. I feel that it will slow down substantially over the next twenty-five years and become a crucial but no longer growing aspect of our global society.

parity 平等；相同

The discovery of life outside of Earth will be (in my view) the greatest scientific/technological event ever, and there is a strong possibility that this will happen by 2040. There also might be a year in which humanity, by working hard to make this century different from all previous centuries, will conquer poverty and starvation, and control the nature of climate change. We have the science and technology to feed, clothe, and maintain all the people on Earth (provided the number of people on Earth doesn't grow rapidly and eventually becomes constant). That would be an accomplishment which we would happily brag about to the new life that we have discovered in a different part of the **galactic** universe.

galactic 银河的

The 2015 world of experimental science will be completely revolutionized in the next four decades by a combination of robotics and computer simulation. Robots will do all sorts of things, ranging from complex chemical synthesis to materials testing, from manipulation of objects to tedious repetitive labours. They will do essentially all of the maintenance and machining necessary in physics and chemistry laboratories and in the commercial world, and they will use 3-D assembly to create (based on computer input) samples of materials, composites, blends, glasses, arrested relaxation materials, and hybrid organic-inorganic entities. Light manipulation and lasers will also be used by robots and by the devices that they will prepare.

One prediction of which I'm reasonably sure is that coffee (or, in exotic situations, **espresso**) will remain the fuel of science in 2040 and well beyond.

espresso 意式浓缩咖啡

In life sciences, astonishing new knowledge will have been created. But major challenges will still remain, and new questions will be asked. Professor Cees Dekker of the University of Delft in the Netherlands is a distinguished physicist who, at the start of the twenty-first century, became deeply interested in biology. He suggests that by 2040 brain scans will be routine and perhaps allow even science fiction–type abilities such as reading thoughts. This is a bit frightening. While information technology and governmental **slipperiness** have essentially removed the right to privacy in most countries in 2015, the last bit of privacy—thinking to ourselves, talking to ourselves, and letting our brains invent and discover new things—will be no longer limited to ourselves but might be read by using brain scans.

slippery 不可靠的

How to connect the concepts of the "mind" and "brain" will be unresolved, and the **Sisyphean** quest for understanding consciousness and mind will continue and remain one of the foremost questions in science (and in philosophy).

Sisyphean 西西弗斯式的；永远做不完的；徒劳的

"Synthetic biology" will be a daily commodity, and microorganisms (because of their adaptive abilities) will be used for many practical applications, from sanitation to colouring paint to **soothing** mosquito bites to creating food. Synthetic biology will have provided artificial cells, whose major applications in the areas of drug delivery and regenerative medicine will have (together with robotics and new

soothe 缓和；减轻

materials) completely changed the face of surgery and many other parts of medicine.

(2,704 words)

❶ Recall

Answer the following questions with the information from the passage.

1. When I. I. Rabi returned home from school, what did his mother ask him?
2. What does the author think of the relationship between science and technology?
3. What will be the principal drivers for scientific exploration?
4. Is tackling the enormous diversity that living creatures on Earth represent a huge challenge for life science?
5. What will be the most awesome event in the history of humankind?
6. What is the prediction that the author is reasonably sure of?

❷ Interpret

Answer the following questions by analysing the passage.

7. At the end of Paragraph 12, the author says, "asking the right question is frequently the most important thing in science." According to the author, why is asking the right question so important in scientific research?
8. At the beginning of Paragraph 14, according to Karl Popper, a true scientific fact has to be falsifiable. But at the end of Paragraph 14, the author quotes from *The Economist*, which describes "the current state of falsifiability as essentially irrelevant." What does the author think of falsifiability in science?

❸ Evaluate & Connect

Answer the following question by relating the passage to your own experience.

9. Apart from the predictions made by the author, what other predictions can you make about the world of science and technology in 2040? Based on your own knowledge and imagination, try to make as many predictions as possible.